FLA[illegible]
FOUL

FLAGRANT FOUL

The tumultuous story of a young man whose life was careening out of control until God's grace intruded on the mayhem.

written by Barry Jones

TATE PUBLISHING & *Enterprises*

Flagrant Foul

Published by Tate Publishing & Enterprises, LLC
127 E. Trade Center Terrace | Mustang, Oklahoma 73064 USA
1.888.361.9473 | www.tatepublishing.com

Tate Publishing is committed to excellence in the publishing industry. The company reflects the philosophy established by the founders, based on Psalm 68:11,
"The Lord gave the word and great was the company of those who published it."

Cover design by Jonathan Lindsey
Interior design by Nathan Harmony

Published in the United States of America

ISBN: 978-1-60696-460-6
1. Biography and Autobiography: Sports: Basketball
2. Inspiration: Motivational: Biography and Autobiography
08.09.25

Dedication

I wish to dedicate this book to my lovely wife, Katrina. Without her love of God and dedication to family, this labor of love would not have been possible. She truly is my sunshine.

Acknowledgments

A project such as this necessarily places undue burdens on lots of people. It would have been impossible without the help and encouragement of my parents. Their hospitality and input have been invaluable. I will always remember the example they set with regard to being willing to step out in faith and follow the path along which God has led them. Furthermore, they took their faith to a higher level when they opened their home to my family of six so we could do the same. Their example reminds me that faith that is alive produces works—my parents' faith is alive and well!

There are so many to remember. Dave Myers for the encouragement to keep on keepin' on with this project and his willingness to get involved in the editing process. As an English teacher who reads countless essays, I'm sure reading this and adding his comments and suggestions was not his idea of fun! Mostly though, I want to say thanks to my wife and kids. I hope one day all of my children will take advantage of this book and learn from their earthly father and his many mistakes. I also trust that this project will help them learn about their Heavenly Father, about his love, his mercy, and his grace. It will be worth it all if my life helps them develop a real and meaningful relationship with their Lord. Katrina has read and re-read this manuscript in an attempt to be supportive. Her advice and suggestions have made this book better. I love you very much, babe!

Lastly, I want to thank the Lord for moving my spirit to undertake something so far out of my comfort zone. Thanks for the strength, the encouragement, and the equipping. Thanks for showing me on a daily basis that I don't have to see the whole picture. I can lean on you because you are the one who sees everything.

Table of Contents

Foreword

The book you are holding is a life-changing story of one man's journey. God transformed an angry, frustrated boy to a strong, Christian man, who now carries the torch to build up a healthy, new generation of young men. Coach Barry Jones, like many who grew up in the shadows of Christian legalism, wondered why anyone would want to have faith in God if all it entailed was following a bunch of rules or "thou shalt nots." Through Barry's younger years, you'll get a sense of how rules without relationships pushed him to the point of denying the faith he had grown up in.

As a way of escaping run-ins with authorities in his teen years, he turned to basketball to deal with his resentful and bitter feelings. This opened up doors and brought him praise that had seemed impossible to a kid with so many problems, including the opportunity to play basketball at the collegiate level. He later eloped with his under-age, high school girlfriend, leaving Michigan for the South, so that they could start a new life together without all the rules and regulations of his family, church, and school.

In his attempt to run away, however, Barry made the most important discovery of his life: neither basketball nor his new marriage could remove the pain of his upbringing or bring him happiness. Through a series of painful experiences during college, Barry found himself recognizing his need for a Savior.

This is a story about how we can never stray too far away from God for him to reach down and save us. This is a story about reconciliation. This is a story of hope. This is a story of redemption. This is Barry's story.

It is my privilege to recommend this book to you. Barry has been a great friend to me, and I have personally witnessed God's transforming power in his life. Barry Jones has experienced God's healing touch in his own life and now has an opportunity to help others along some of life's more difficult roads. You'll understand God's redemptive grace on a much more personal level than perhaps you ever have before by the time you have finished reading this.

Dave Myers
Writer and contributor for sportsmensdevotional.com
Men's Ministry Leader, Word Of Life Baptist Church

Preface

Flagrant Foul is the story of my life, written to follow two journeys: the chronological life and times of a young boy growing into manhood and, more importantly, the spiritual transformation that happened as a result of the many mistakes and wrong turns along the way.

I tried to begin by drawing the reader into a world of legalism and control. These rules and codes prevailed over my family and were a direct result of the influence of our church and the pastor. This performance-driven environment began to shape me at an early age, and the lack of freedom eventually drove me to a form of underground resistance.

My intention was to demonstrate how the issues that bubbled forth and exploded like a volcano in my teenage years didn't happen overnight. In fact, as I got older and began to connect the dots between my family's "religion" and my lack of freedom, the underground resistance became full-throated rebellion.

This rebellion, of course, had many far-reaching consequences. *Flagrant Foul* paints a graphic picture of the results of trying to fight my way through life. However, my objective was not to depress the reader with story after story of broken relationships or missed opportunities. The purpose was to encourage others who may be encountering similar situations in their own lives. Without God intersecting my life and without his grace making a way where there seemed to be no way, my life would have been, as the Greeks called it, a tragedy.

But God *did* intervene on my behalf, and he has taken this broken clay pot and made it useful again. His grace has worked miracles of reversal, of restoration, and of reconciliation. If he can do this in my life, then how could I "hide my light under a bushel" and not share the hope that he can do the same in other people's lives as well?

PART I

Get Me Out Of Here!

The pastor was just getting warmed up. He'd already spent considerable time outlining the evils of television and every other form of media. Then, as if realizing that none of his congregation had a TV anyway, he moved on. Ladies were exhorted to dress modestly. I don't recall the working definition he used to explain modesty, but he had a long list of "suggestions" they should follow. I stole a quick glance at the women in the next pew, sitting there in long, floor-length skirts, buttoned up collars, long sleeves, hair past their waists, and no make-up. I remember wondering why none of them seemed pretty to me.

Lots of topics were covered that day. Men were to rule over their households with "authority," and women were to submit without asking questions. Kids were a blessing from the Lord. Something was even said about a man being blessed if his "quiver" was full of them. I knew better than to risk taking another look around this time, but it occurred to me that our church must have been the most blessed church around because we sure had lots of full quivers.

The King James Bible was, apparently, the only translation authorized by God himself. Little League baseball was a tool of the devil to corrupt the children. What? I woke up from my trance on the last note. There it was: the official position of the church. I wasn't going to get to play baseball that spring after all. Dad had been pondering whether or not to let me play, and he'd made the mistake, I thought, of asking the pastor for his input. We just got it.

I was raised in the late seventies and early eighties in a strict, Christian home in Ligonier, Indiana. My parents had been converted out of the hippie culture when I was very young. During college, they'd traveled to California during the summers, living on the beach and listening to Hendrix and Joplin. They had even been to Woodstock. After their conversion, they set out to pour the same passion into their new-found faith.

As a family, we attended every kid's nightmare of a church. I can still remember that pastor ranting from the pulpit. I can still see the veins bulging from his forehead. When he got really worked up, he would pound with his fist on the pulpit and start jumping around screaming and turning red. I was convinced one day he'd die of a brain aneurism right there on the platform. It was truly a sight to behold.

Grace Bible Church seemed to major on one philosophical premise: to be separate. We were taught to be different. Girls were not permitted to wear slacks, cut their hair, or wear makeup. Boys couldn't wear shorts or wear their hair over their ears. We were taught not to mingle with "heathens." This meant community sports teams were out, public school was a big no-no, and having friends outside the "flock" was discouraged. The pastor said that TV was "the devil's tool" to do something. I don't remember what. Radio was bad, too, because the influence of rock music would surely damn our souls.

Parents were taught to discipline their kids severely. In our home, that meant spankings with a hickory board. Somebody had given my dad an endless supply of hickory planks that he cut into four-foot long "rods of correction." I remember some legendary "board meetings" where dad had to temporarily suspend action in order to replace a broken paddle.

Mercy was not a concept I remember hearing much about as a child. Every social situation was covered with an extensive list of dos and don'ts. Naturally, this environment was terribly exciting for any youngster in which to grow up.

Of course, as luck would have it, Grace Bible Church also had a school. It wasn't enough that we had to endure the church all day Sunday and every Wednesday night. We were institutionalized every Monday through Friday in what had to be the educational equivalent of the Soviet model of instruction.

In an unfortunate twist of fate for us, that very same pastor served as the school superintendent, too. He was sure to hire like-minded, twisted, evil, single women to carry out his edicts in the classrooms. There are many memories I have of that school, but the one that stands out is the fact we never had recess or physical education. The school was so small we didn't have to change classes in the traditional sense, so we just sat there in our desks all day. The only time we could stretch our legs was the happy occasion when we were given permission to go to the bathroom.

One year, the school scheduled a field day. I almost hyperventilated from excitement. Before that day was over, I hit a girl upside the head while swinging a bat, knocked three or four boys over while trying to catch the soccer ball in a rousing game of "three dollars," and pushed several kids onto the ground while playing tag. All were accidents, due to my overzealous enthusiasm mixing toxically with an overabundance of energy. At the end of the day, because the teacher said I didn't work and play well with others, I ended up sitting alone in the classroom, dejectedly listening to my classmates play a rousing game of speedball without me.

Because of this Gestapo-like existence, I had been deathly afraid to voice my displeasure with our situation. I was well aware of the consequences of any such action. Instead, I began to rebel quietly as I got older. I remember sneaking off when I was eleven or twelve and using lawn-mowing money to buy a small radio. This may sound like an exaggeration, but to a boy who had never seen or heard anything over the airwaves before, that radio was an eye-opener for me. I mostly listened to Yankees games, but I also began developing a fondness for country-western music. I couldn't get enough of Merle Haggard, Willie Nelson, and Hank Williams, Jr.

I also remember going away to church camp one summer and taking some scissors along so I could cut off my pants and look like the other boys come swim time. I remember vaguely that all this standing out and "being the light of the world" was beginning to get old. It seemed like the saltier I was, the weirder I felt.

One day in the middle of my eighth grade year, on the way home from school, I finally blurted out to my mother, "I just can't stand it anymore!" I was crying when I said it, and I believe she knew I was about as serious as I had ever been.

I was beginning to be a discipline problem at school because I couldn't sit still. I had a lot of pent-up energy, and it seemed to get me into trouble on a continual basis. We were on the *Pace* program. The *Pace* program is a series of workbooks in all the various subjects. Each student works at his or her own pace, and the objective is to finish the series of workbooks before the end of the school year.

Each of us was separated by wooden cubicles, and that was our day. We were supposed to work on our *Pace* booklets and not bother anyone around us. I can't even begin to tell you how crazy that environment drove me. My method of coping was to rush through the workbooks as fast as I could, and then hope and pray the teacher had some errands for me to run so I could get out and be free. Sometimes, the teacher would make me run laps around the building because I was becoming such a distraction to those around me. Either way, I didn't mind.

It was after one of these mind-numbing experiences on a school day that I finally blurted out my true feelings about the school and the church. Fortunately, the way I remember it, my mother listened, and I felt emboldened to dump all my frustrations out at that moment. I went on and on, and by the time I was finished, I remember my mother was crying, too.

It wasn't long after that my parents announced to the family that we were moving to Angola, Indiana. I was excited as we drove along to see our new house. I remember thinking that I would live in an old shoe if it meant I didn't have to go back to Grace Bible Church and Syracuse Christian School. We moved during the middle of the school year. Thus, I finished one week at Syracuse Christian School and began the next at Grace Baptist Academy.

Choosing My "Team"

Immediately after my arrival at Grace Baptist Academy, I tried out for the basketball team. Growing up in Indiana, it would be easy to assume that all boys do nothing but play basketball. That may be the case for most, but not for me. Syracuse Christian School hadn't had recess or physical education, so why would it have had an athletic program? That would have meant competition against other schools, which would mean mingling with heathens wearing shorts!

While trying out for the team, I became instantly aware of my athletic shortcomings. I was horrible. Furthermore, I had never worn shorts before. As I tiptoed out of the locker room with my new gym shorts on, I became cognizant of my social limitations.

The gym was full of people, and all of them, as if on cue, turned to gawk at the nerd with the white, bony legs standing there looking like the emperor with no clothes on. Fortunately for me, the school had a no-cut policy, so I was on the team, but barely.

Grace Baptist Academy had standards, as all Christian schools do. It's important to note, though, that these standards were much more lenient than to what I was accustomed. Where others may have felt restricted by Grace's standards, I felt liberated. I felt free! This little dose of freedom, however, did to me what it does to many people who have been under lock and key. It causes them to do things they might ordinarily not do. In my case, I latched onto the "cool" kids at Grace and began "catching up" on all the things an eighth-grade boy should know.

Of course, as is often the case in high school, the cool kids were the troublemakers. I'm sure they looked at me as some kind of peculiar plaything, a toy to be exploited and used, but that was okay by me. I thought any attention I could get from them was good for me. And so it went. It wasn't long before my friends were the rebels in school.

I'm sure my parents looked at their oldest son and thought they'd made a big mistake by leaving the safe confines of the old for the relative freedom of the new. Things were not working out like they'd hoped.

Instead of being grateful for the newfound freedom, I wanted more. So, my parents reverted to what they knew. They attempted to re-create the Grace Bible Church environment in our home in order to maintain some degree of control over me.

In our house, my father was the enforcer. His job often had him out of town for up to four days at a time, during which I'd invariably do something to deserve being punished. Later that night, during their phone conversation, Mom would inform Dad of "Barry's latest escapade(s)." He'd tell her to "ground him in his room" until he returned, and then "he'd take care of me." I believe that's when I was first introduced to the concept of "double jeopardy."

I'd sit in my room for three days or so, waiting for the "real" punishment to come. I vividly recall some of those spankings being marathon sessions. They always started with dad telling me how many whacks I was due. Then "the rule" would kick in. Every time I fell or tried to deflect the blow by putting my hand behind me defensively, another whack would be added to my total. One time, I was "assigned" fifty whacks. I must have fallen a thousand times because we never were able to finish the spanking that day. I just remember crawling back to my room and lying very still.

Naturally, I grew to dread my father. Every time I saw him, it seemed I was in some kind of trouble. In his younger days, my father was an austere, strict disciplinarian. He was also physically intimidating. He was six-foot, six-inches tall and incredibly strong. I loved him and I knew he loved me. Nevertheless, I grew to hate his presence.

So the battle lines were drawn. It was me versus my parents. I was growing older, getting bigger and stronger, so I became less terrified of my father's presence. I was also growing bolder as I became exposed to new things. I would act out, and my father would come down hard on me. Instead of changing my behavior, I would continue and so would he.

My mother's role was to be the peacemaker or the instigator, depending on her mood. She could doom or delight with her reports to dad. We fought over issues like my music, my friends, my clothes, my hair, and my jobs, all seemingly insignificant now, but important at the time.

During the next few years though, the regard I had for my parents, especially their faith, was becoming jaded. I was hardening. I was looking at both teams and choosing which one I wanted to play for. And it wasn't theirs.

Discovering a Dream

Meanwhile, the experience of playing on the basketball team had changed me. It had opened my eyes to a whole new world. I had finally found something I could become good at, with a little work. My father was a graduate of Notre Dame, and he had always stressed academics. I must have been a constant source of disappointment for him because school was definitely not my thing.

In fact, with the exception of our mutual passion for Notre Dame football, I didn't like many things he liked. My father loved classical music. He took us to symphonies and concerts when I was young. He even made me play piano for ten years and was never more proud than when I successfully performed the *Moonlight Sonata* at my last recital. Later on, when I turned sixteen, he allowed me to finally quit. I'm sure it broke his heart. He knew I was listening to country and western music. It must have driven him nuts, which is what I wanted.

He also loved to work in the wood shop making end tables and bookshelves. I couldn't think of an enterprise more boring and uneventful than nailing, sawing, painting, and gluing. He'd haul me down to the basement to engage in a little father-son time, but I was miserable.

Our interests always seemed to be at odds until I discovered basketball. He had played in high school and even tried out in college. I had watched him play many times down at the local high school and other places and always admired how good he was. In those days, he could run and jump exceptionally well for a big man. He had exceptional timing on defense, which he demonstrated many times, when, in his words, "little guys" would come into "his world," and he'd have to reject their shots with a resounding swat!

When I tried out in eighth grade, it was my first time to play on my own, and I loved it. I started working hard at it and discovered I had inherited some athletic ability and natural talent for the sport after all. It was the first time I discovered something that could set me apart, something that made me special. A kid never forgets a moment like that.

It was because of basketball my father made a decision I never thought he'd make. Grace Baptist Academy had a basketball team, but no true coaching. It was a typical Christian school. Always short on resources, the school had to cut corners, and coaches were hard to come by.

My earliest recollection was of a coach who, after he got off his shift at the DANA factory, would bring a John Wooden book to practice. We'd all huddle around as he tried to figure out the drills.

My father had watched me work for hours out back on the court, and he'd evidently noticed an improvement. I practically lived at Tri-State University's athletic complex down the street, working on my game and trying to play with the college guys. I decided that one day I was going to play basketball in college. I remember announcing my dream at the dinner table one evening.

When we first came to the Academy, it had a good team.

The coach was demanding, and there were quite a few talented players. Before I began ninth grade, however, the church split, and all that talent left and went somewhere else. Furthermore, the coach was fired. I literally went from worst to first overnight. I had worked hard over the summer to improve, but, realistically, in a normal situation, I would have still been a "bottom feeder" player.

My dad had seen me improve during my freshman and sophomore years. He had played basketball in high school too, so he knew I was destined to fall short in my quest unless I got under some good coaching and faced better competition. He waited a couple of years, hoping the situation at Grace would improve, but it never did. Time was running out, so he said I could go to Angola High School at the beginning of my junior year. I was thrilled.

At Angola High, I began to make new friends and drift farther away from my family. In fact, I remember consciously trying my best to stay away from home as much as possible. By this point, fitting in was not as hard. I had it down pat. I was beginning to make friends in my own right, and by virtue of my athletic ability, I was now in a socially acceptable clique, the "jocks."

My world was opening up, and I was loving it. I had discovered a new friend in basketball. For me, it had provided the escape I so desired from the Christian schools I'd grown up in.

I loved playing. The more I played, the better I got. I began to seriously dream about things that would have seemed unimaginable just a few short years ago. The years of frustration and misery were behind me, and basketball had become my ticket to a bright future.

Meanwhile, as I assimilated into a new culture, I purposefully tried to leave my own family behind. Some of it was probably natural for a teenage boy, but I became more and more conscious of how strange my family was. At least to my new way of thinking, they were stuck in a world I'd left behind. There would be no going back. All I needed was an issue with which I could assert my independence.

Love or Something Like It

I took a new job at a grocery store near the end of my sophomore year and met a girl named Denise. I had never been in love before, but I've since observed others in the state of "first love." I can assure you that all the foolishness I've observed in others with this particular malady was evident in my relationship with Denise. I was head-over-heels for her and would do anything to be with her.

My parents took a stand, saying I would not be permitted to date her because she was not a Christian. I immediately claimed that I was not a Christian either, so what did it matter? My parents didn't budge. It quickly became apparent that the independence I wanted would be fought over the issue of a girlfriend.

I began secretly meeting with Denise behind my parents' backs. They would catch me on occasion and punish me accordingly. I'd sneak out again or violate the terms of the punishment, and on it would go.

There was something about my personality that made this scenario unlikely to continue. I was hardheaded and obtuse. I was also outspoken and stubborn. The sneaking around and lying to cover my tracks was getting old. Combine my personality with the natural tendency of any adolescent male who is sowing his wild oats to eventually take a public stand, and it's not hard to extrapolate the situation and foresee trouble down the road.

During my junior year, I was grounded and decided to sneak out one night to meet up with Denise. My father was out of town on business, so I felt my mom would be easy pickings. As far as I knew, I had been successful on my little "end-around."

However, when I returned home from school the next evening, all of my clothes and other belongings were lying in the front yard. Mom had kicked me out of the house. Evidently she'd seen me as I pedaled my Schwinn down the hill the night before. I had no money and no place to go.

That night, I snuck into our basement and slept on the floor. The next morning, my plan was to beat everybody out of bed and go off to school. But I overslept and my dad, who had returned from his trip, found me. He'd gotten the full scoop from my mother and was obviously miffed.

When he discovered me sleeping on the basement floor, he chased me out of the house yelling something to the effect of, "If I catch you back here again, I'll take a ball-bat to you." So, while running down the street, I decided it'd probably be wise to make living arrangements with Chris, one of my friends at school.

It was only a month or two before I violated the terms of my new living arrangements. My friends' parents had told me that as long as I was truthful with them, they'd treat me with the same respect they gave their own son. Of course, they had rules in their house, too, and they explained them to me. However, I wasn't about to abide by anybody's rules, especially if those rules prevented unlimited access to my girlfriend.

Before long, I was in trouble for sneaking out again, so they told me I could not see Denise for two weeks. To a teenager in love, that is an eternity. I called my folks and asked for a second chance. My father had taken me out for ice cream while I was living with Chris and his family because he wanted to reconcile. I'd brushed him off because things had been going well for me at the time. Now, though, things weren't in my favor, so I made the call.

I lied, saying I was sorry for everything. Of course, I said nothing about my situation at Chris' house. Maybe they knew and maybe they didn't, but they threw their arms around me anyway and killed the fatted calf to celebrate their prodigal son's return. In the words of Pete Rose, "It was all hats and horns!"

Upon my return, my father told me that all the old rules still applied. I ignored him, of course. Gradually, I'm sure it became apparent to my parents that my return had not meant a change of heart on my part. I just picked up where I'd left off.

One evening, I was talking to Denise on the phone, and Dad caught me. He told me to get off the phone, and I refused. He grabbed the phone and knocked me down. It was on. The phone was dangling and Denise could hear everything. I was screaming and cussing at my dad, and he was taking out his frustrations on me. All my brothers and sisters witnessed it, and my mom was running to and fro, yelling, "Hit him again, Mark!"

I was furious. I left the house and went to the police station. Since there were no obvious marks, the police declined to file a report and I had to go home. By this point, the entire house was on edge. I refused to talk to or even acknowledge my parents. They hibernated in their room.

A few nights later, I snuck out and took the car. I had never done that before. I met up with Denise, and we had a great time. My parents were at my grandfather's house watching a Notre Dame football game, so I figured I could rendezvous with my girlfriend and still get the car back before my parents returned.

Naturally, I stayed too late, and my parents returned to find one of their cars missing. When I got back and saw the car they'd been gone in, I kept on driving. Thoughts of running away entered my head. I stayed out all night, driving around trying to think of my options. In the morning, I went to see my parents' pastor. I figured that if anyone could give me some mercy, it would be him. He called my parents, and all parties agreed that I should stay with him for a night or two.

It was during my junior year that social services began taking an interest in my situation. During this time, I had continued going to school as if nothing was happening. However, I was wearing the same clothes every day. Sometimes I'd show up with marks on my face, and I never had money for lunch.

My parents' next-door neighbor also happened to be a teacher at the high school, and I think she'd alerted some folks to my predicament. Anyway, I believe they'd had their eye on me for some time, so I was called to the office to meet with a counselor. We talked, and I told her briefly what was going on.

It was decided that my parents needed to find a neutral

place for me to live. One winter day, they picked me up from the pastor's house and drove me to Indianapolis, Indiana. When we stopped, we were out in the country and a long way from anything resembling civilization.

It didn't take long for my "weird-o-meter," which had been so acutely developed during my Grace Bible days, to start going bonkers. I was at a huge, old, brick building in the middle of a field. There were kids everywhere doing work: odd jobs like cutting wood, stacking wood, shoveling sawdust, and picking up sticks. Adults were standing around watching the kids work. I smelled a rat.

My parents took me inside and brought me to an office. I was looking at everything and everybody, and the place just dripped with strange vibes. I saw kids staring at me with wide eyes like I'd just arrived from another planet or something. As we met with the director, my worst fears were confirmed.

They had brought me to a group home. I was going to be institutionalized and taken to the Dominican Republic to be a missionary, building log huts for the natives. Evidently, all new "recruits" were taken to there to perform these tasks until the life had been sufficiently sapped from them, and they were no longer a flight risk.

I'll never forget one of the bodyguards taking me into a room and asking me if I wanted to be a part of this enterprise. You can imagine my response. He said, "Look out that window." I looked just in time to see my parents driving away into the night. I couldn't believe it. I vowed they'd never keep me there, and they all laughed and said something to the effect of, "Everybody says that when they first get here."

That night, five men and I loaded into a car and began

the drive to Fort Wayne, Indiana. They were taking me to a psychiatrist to be tested. Institutions like this required a mental exam to be conducted on minors whose parents would be turning over guardianship to the group home.

After looking at twenty-seven 3x5 cards with different variations of the same theme, flying bats with blood and other gory images, the good doctor was convinced that I was sufficiently "homicidal and suicidal," meeting the state's requirements.

As we exited the building, I made my break. I ran down back streets and alleys. They chased on foot and in the car. They called the police to assist, and several times it appeared they were going to catch me.

At one time, two of them caught and pinned me against a tree. One held me high around the shoulders, and the other held me low around the knees. I was begging them to let me go when a police car pulled up. Two officers jumped out with their flashlights. I don't remember what happened next, but somehow I got away. I later found out that in the struggle, I'd beaten up two men. I never found out the circumstances of how that happened. I don't know what happened to the cops, either. Part of me still believes my guardian angel took up for me that night and protected me from that crazy group home.

Regardless, the next thing I remember is that I was free and clear, walking the streets of Fort Wayne, Indiana at 11:00 p.m. I walked for an hour or so, trying to put some distance between the posse and me. I found a McDonald's where I could clean myself up.

Fighting Mad

It was snowing that night, so I began looking for some kind of shelter. A friendly doorman at a theater let me stand in the lobby after making a phone call to Denise. She told me that my parents had already called and informed her she'd never see me again.

She and her parents drove to Fort Wayne that night and picked me up. It was a night I'll never forget. It was quiet in the car all the way home. I couldn't sleep. I was angry. I kept thinking about how I'd gotten to this point. All I wanted was my freedom, freedom to make judgments, good and bad. Freedom to make up my own mind. I couldn't believe that "normal" behavior by other sixteen-year-olds was considered deviant in my household. One thing was sure of: I was going to face my folks in the morning, and they were going to pay for their treachery.

The next morning, Denise's mother took me home. Her parents had decided to ask my parents to sign over legal guardianship. I thought that sounded cool. When we arrived at my home, my mother was the only one there. She cried when she saw me, but I was cold. She told me they'd left me at the home because they didn't know what else to do with me. It was at that point that she told me, "Nobody wants you."

Denise's mother spoke up and said they'd be willing to

take me if they could have full custody. My mother agreed and that was that. I loaded up my belongings, and off we went. A couple months later, my parents moved the family to Toledo, Ohio, to follow my father's new job. Meanwhile, because Denise lived in a different school zone, I transferred from Angola High School to the second school of my junior year, Prairie Heights High School.

It would be easy to think that I was finally happy. I wasn't. Deep down, I was sad. I loved my family, even my parents. We just couldn't get along. I had made a choice, and yet, I was not altogether happy with the consequences.

Ironically, all of this turmoil had made playing basketball impossible. The very reason I'd been sent to Angola High School was to pursue my basketball dream. I had gotten caught up in the pixie dust of young love and turned my back on my passion. I was forced to work to help pay my way. One day, in an unusual moment of clarity, I realized that I had given up a lot to be with this girl. I hoped she'd be worth it. My family lived hours away, and despite our differences, I still craved their acceptance. I wanted to make my parents proud, just like any other kid.

Denise's family did their best to accommodate me, but they were different. I was unaccustomed to many things. It wasn't long before I began to withdraw to myself. Because of our close proximity, I began to discover things about Denise that made me a little uneasy. I remember learning that she had been born out of wedlock seventeen years earlier and how that scared me. When we first met, she was pretty wise to the world compared to me and had, in short order, taught me the ropes as well. Once the sexual line had been crossed, however, I began to feel insecure about her history with other guys and became quite possessive. Of course, she didn't like that and things started to disintegrate.

She was very much like her mother, and I was uncomfortable with that because I knew history would probably repeat itself. Little by little, the excitement of our relationship began to cool. I'm sure she was a symbol of my resistance to my parents. Once they were out of the equation, her allure was partly diminished. We began to fight about things.

One night during work, I found out that one of my co-workers had been flirting with Denise. I was not known as a fighter. Growing up, I'd been in my share of dust-ups like most boys, but I didn't have the reputation as a brawler. Something had changed in me, though. I was angry and becoming short-tempered.

That night, I lost it. While on the clock and in front of customers, I pulled my co-worker out of his car and beat him senseless. He was a lineman on the football team and was known as one of the tough guys at the school. But that night, he didn't know what hit him. He had come to the store to pick up his paycheck and didn't know I was waiting to ambush him. Everyone looked at me afterward with an expression of disbelief. I still recall the anger that came out of me that night as I straddled him and beat his head with my fists. He couldn't go to school for weeks because of the damage to his face. Amazingly enough, I didn't get fired because my boss had been out back burning boxes. I cleaned up and went back to bagging groceries.

Finally, things fell apart completely when I intercepted a note Denise had written to a friend, in which she was discussing the possibility of not taking her birth control in order to get herself pregnant and force my hand.

That was enough for me. I had just received a phone call from my mother asking me if I'd like to come to Toledo and visit for a weekend. I called her back after I discovered Denise's note and took her up on the invitation. The next day, my parents picked me up.

I had a good weekend in Toledo. By that point cooler heads had prevailed, and my parents had decided to let sleeping dogs lie. I had grown my hair out to show who was boss. I'm sure they weren't real keen on it, but to their credit, no one said anything.

At the end of the weekend, I asked my parents if I could move back. Both sides had endured a lot, and I felt that things would be different this time. I could tell that they knew I could not be handled like before because I'd walk away. I'd done it before, and I wouldn't hesitate to do it again.

I also felt things were never going to be the same at Denise's. I was never going to be able to play basketball while living there, and I desperately wanted to play again. I thought about these things all weekend and finally came to the conclusion that if I wanted to play ball that badly, I'd have to suck it up and take the chance that my parents had chilled out considerably and would give me some space.

They were open to it, and we all drove back to Indiana to get my things. That was the last time I ever saw Denise. It was weird. I had fought so hard for the right to be with her, and then I walked away of my own choosing. Life has since taught me that Denise was not a first love, rather a symbol of my desire to be free. The interesting thing, though, was that I'd achieved that freedom I wanted so desperately, and yet I found it came at a very high cost, a price I found to be unsatisfactory.

The following week, everything nearly exploded in our faces again. My parents wanted to enroll me at the local Christian school. I wasn't sure about it. Emmanuel Baptist High School was a nice place, and I'm sure I could have made it through. However, I had too many bad memories of anything "Christian." The administrator explained to me that they would only accept me if I signed their code of conduct and expressed a desire to be there. I agreed and later kicked myself for it.

Everyone was nice, but I could feel myself slipping back into the old habit of acting out on everybody's expectations of me. One thing I had noticed was that in a "Christian" environment, I was considered something of an outlaw. Because I felt it was pointless to try to overcome that prejudice, I'd simply act out in a way to confirm everybody's beliefs about me. However, I'd also found that in a secular setting, I was looked upon as a good guy with standards and beliefs not normally found in teenagers. In one setting I was looked down on, and in the other I was looked up to.

As I walked around Emmanuel that first day with my new haircut, I felt the eyes and knew that behind the friendliness was a cautionary edge. I wanted none of it. I asked a teacher for permission to use the bathroom and just kept walking, right out of Emmanuel Baptist High School during third period, never to return. I had only lasted two and a half periods in my third school that year.

The school called my parents, and everybody rushed home for the big pow-wow. My dad was angry. My mom was resigned. I was flippant. “There’s no way I’m going to that school,” I said to Dad. He threatened to send me off to the group home again, and at that, I got mad. I told him he’d never see me if he ever brought it up again. That night, I called Denise and asked if I could come back. Her mother said no.

Senioritis

The next morning, my father enrolled me in my fourth school that year, Whiteford High School. It was very small. From the moment I walked in the doors, though, I felt at home. I had grown to my full six-foot, five-inches of height and had an athletic build. I suppose in a small school, things like that get noticed. We registered for classes, and the principal rushed me down to the elementary wing to meet the varsity boys' basketball coach.

I'll never forget meeting John Rice for the first time. He was the physical education teacher for the elementary school. He was short, with skinny legs, a barrel chest, a round face, and a huge mop of curly hair, Shirley Temple curly. It was almost an afro. From the time I met him, I knew I'd like him because he cussed like a sailor. I learned words in our first conversation that I'd never heard before. Something about him just made me smile.

We talked for a while, and he probably wasn't excited about my prospects once he heard my basketball background. I hadn't been able to play at all my junior year and had only had two prior years of experience at a rinky-dink Christian school. That gave me another reason to like him immediately. When I mentioned my Christian school background, he just sneered and rolled his eyes. He asked me with a trace of sarcasm if I would be allowed to practice on prayer meeting night. I thought it was funny.

Nevertheless, he offered me a chance to try out that afternoon during practice. After five minutes of practicing with the team, Coach Rice had changed his mind. I was going to prove useful after all. In fact, he and the others who had gathered to watch the tryout seemed giddy. I was happy to be playing ball again. I finished the season that year as a practice player and slowly began to carve out a niche for myself going into my senior year.

At that point, my senior year was the happiest year of my life. My parents and I stayed out of each other's way. I did go to church with them on Sundays, but that was it. I probably wasn't at home more than two weeks out of the entire year. I had made friends quickly at Whiteford, and basketball kept me occupied otherwise.

My life followed true to form that year. It always seemed that when I was in Christian schools, I tended to hang out with the dregs of society. When I was in public schools, though, I gravitated to good, solid, and more often than not, Christian guys. One such friend was Keith Parsons.

I met Keith during basketball practice at Whiteford during the first week I was there, and we soon became best friends. He took me to his house one night, and I became a part of his family. They had a swimming pool outside and a game room in their basement. They had a basketball court with lights in front. They even had a big screen TV with a satellite dish. Most importantly, they always had lots of food. I learned all about brown cow and bean dip that year.

Interestingly enough, the Parsons attended Emmanuel

Baptist Church and were strong Christians. They kept their mouths shut around me and never judged me though, and I always appreciated that. Keith hadn't had a lot of friends either during his high school years, so naturally, his parents were happy to nurture the relationship in spite of my rocky background, as long as we did it in their presence. Through the Parsons, God provided an oasis away from home where I would be safe. I wasn't with my family, but I was with the next best thing.

I'm sure my parents and the Parsons communicated often on the sly, but that was okay with me because the Parsons never pushed me in any direction. They loved me like a son. They had such a profound influence on me because they showed love without judgment.

Academically, I wallowed in mediocrity as usual. I had long since given up trying to get good grades. I hadn't done poorly my first two years of high school, but my junior year had almost ruined me. However, one positive had emerged from the ordeal. Because I'd gone to so many schools, I'd taken a lot of courses that I would normally not take until my senior year.

Consequently, I only had a couple required classes to take. All my other classes would be electives. My schedule was a joke. I took a couple sections of art, as well as family living, home economics, choir, gym, etc. I even volunteered as a gym aid for Coach Rice so I could shoot baskets for the entire period. Naturally, I was bored in these classes, so I was mischievous.

Athletically, I prospered. Whiteford had a strong basketball tradition, and Coach Rice was a legend. He was the first adult figure who I can remember saying the things he said or doing the things he did to me without me quitting or firing back in some manner. He pushed me, and I ate it up.

We had our moments, but he knew what buttons to push. One of the great things he did was giving me rope, and lots of it. I never played for another coach who gave me the kind of freedom he did. We had a great year. I was named First Team All-State in Michigan, and the team was ranked in the top five in the state all year. Things were looking up.

Basketball even helped my relationship with my parents. For the first time, I was doing something they could be proud of. I was getting lots of attention for something productive rather than destructive. That season helped bridge many hurts in the short term. They would come up again later, but for that year, everything was okay again.

I dated around my senior year. Coming from monogamy with Denise, I was eager to stretch my legs and sow some wild oats. I wasn't into any commitments, mind you, just good, old-fashioned fun. I'd date one girl, then another. Mostly, I aimed my sights at the younger girls, the ones with stars in their eyes because I was a basketball player. I stayed away from girls who seemed like they had their act together because I knew they'd see right through me. My main interest that year was common to most seniors: having fun.

After graduation, I visited my grandfather for the Fourth of July holiday. He lived in Syracuse, Indiana, near my old school. I drove by to see it and a flood of memories came back. I remembered the hatred I felt for that place. It was so vivid I could taste the feeling in my mouth. A few people I vaguely recognized were standing out in the parking lot, so I stopped. I'm not sure what drew me in, but I felt I had to stop.

I got out of the car and they all looked at me. It was then that I realized I was wearing shorts with no shirt. I had a chain around my neck, and I'd driven up playing loud music on my car stereo. I'm sure I personified the devil in their eyes. As I got closer, I recognized one of them as the pastor whom I'd grown to despise. All the old fears came rushing back. I was just getting my courage up when I looked more closely at him.

He looked different. When I was young, he looked robust, always overweight, but healthy otherwise. Now he looked gaunt. His face looked old and tired. He seemed to have gotten shorter, and his clothes hung on his frame like a scarecrow. His voice had changed, too. He recognized me, and, instead of bellowing like he used to, he mustered up a feeble, "Hi, Barry." All the bitterness left me. I was instantly embarrassed at my appearance and started making excuses. He waved me off and never made a point of it.

We talked and caught up. He wanted to know about the family, my parents especially. He told me he was sick and didn't know how much time he had left. I wanted to hate him and tell him a lot of things. I just couldn't. I drove away, found a place to pull off the road, and cried for a good while. I don't know why, but I felt better after it was over. I never saw him again, as he died a short while later.

After graduating in 1989, I wanted desperately to go to college to play ball. My grades were so poor, though, that I was in a position where I'd have to beg someone to take a chance on me. I decided to enroll at the University of Toledo for one year to get my grades up and then try to transfer. Little did I know how much my life would change during that one year.

Beauty and the Beast

Instead of improving my academic record, I promptly flunked three of my first four college courses and withdrew. I was working instead of going to class, and it showed. I continued my high school study habits in college and found that college professors don't give extra credit.

Meanwhile, after going through one girlfriend after another during my senior year, I had begun to notice someone who might seem to be an unlikely fit for me considering my history.

I first met Katrina Martin the weekend I left Denise's house to visit my family in Toledo. She was my sister's best friend and happened to be at the house when I walked in. I noticed her immediately because she was very pretty. My sister and I were close, so we spent a lot of time together that weekend. Since Katrina was staying with my sister, she was forced to hang out with me too.

I'm sure she wasn't impressed with me then, not my appearance, my vocabulary, or my personality. I'm not sure there was anything about me that was remotely attractive. It didn't take me long to figure out she was a "do-gooder" with the right "Christian" pedigree. I naturally lumped her in with all the rest of the Christian hypocrites I'd known through the years and wrote her off as one of "them."

During the remainder of my junior year and my senior

year, Katrina and I saw a lot of each other, but not intentionally, mind you. It seemed that every time I did make an appearance at my house, Katrina was there. When I went to youth group at Emmanuel, she was there. I began making sport of her. I'd make fun of her because she was naïve, which made her an easy target.

She was the happiest individual I'd ever met. This bothered me, so I made it my mission to make her as miserable as I was. She and my sister loved to play the piano and sing. Of course, they'd pick the worst times to serenade the rest of us. It would usually be during the middle of a Notre Dame football game. I would come in and lay into them about being too loud or sounding horrible. It didn't matter. I'd find something.

My sister could take it. She was used to me and shook off my manners easily. Katrina was delicate, and it upset her. When I noticed that, it made it that much more fun. I'd actually look forward to seeing her, and then I'd try to publicly embarrass her. It got to a point that she told my sister she wouldn't come over anymore if I was there. That was fine by me.

I felt this way about her because she seemed to represent everything I hated. She was the golden girl of Emmanuel Baptist Church and school. She sang solos at church, was very active in the youth group, and seemed to be the poster child for all that's right about Christian young people. I called her a fraud.

During one event my senior year, we were sitting through another monotonous service during which the pastor had made one of those typical emotional appeals to all the young people in the church. He pleaded for all the teens who wanted to demonstrate their commitment to the Lord to stand up and walk down front.

Of course, every teenager in the place flooded the front of the auditorium and stood there with all due piety. I watched as several of my buddies ran down front with the other sheep. Kids were practically tripping and falling over each other like there was limited space on the good spaceship heaven-bound. It was unbelievable.

Naturally, I stood my ground. My parents were probably shamed by my refusal to follow the pied piper down front, but I didn't care. You could look around the auditorium and see all the parents beaming with pride as their children rededicated their lives.

Later that night, Katrina was visiting my sister, and I started picking on her for joining the other sheep down front. I laid it on pretty thick. She argued with me and claimed that it was not a ploy as I had cynically suggested. She almost started crying as she professed her pure motives. I laughed at her and told her she wouldn't know what commitment was if it bit her in the butt. After all, what stress could she have in her life? We left it at that, and she went home convinced I was the reincarnation of Nero. I thought she was a phony-baloney.

Sometime during the year after I graduated from high school and flunked out of college, something happened that dramatically changed my feelings toward Katrina. She had been working throughout the summer on an island in Lake Erie as a camp counselor for Camp Patmos. One night, one of the girls in her cabin found her on the floor unconscious. The camp administrator called for help, and she took a life-flight to a hospital in Toledo. It was fogged in that night, so finding a pilot and a plane took time. Enough time in fact, that her parents got word that she probably wasn't going to make it.

I was playing basketball in our driveway the next day when I heard the news. I probably didn't show it, but I was upset. I hoped she'd be all right. That was the first sympathetic thought I'd ever had toward Katrina. She'd been diagnosed with spinal meningitis and was in a coma for three days. It was touch and go for a while.

Later that week, I was in the shower when I heard a knock. My mother shouted through the door that Katrina had come out of her coma. She said something else that I couldn't hear, so I went to the door. She told me that the youth pastor from Emmanuel had just called and asked for me to come to the hospital. I thought that was odd. I certainly didn't have a meaningful relationship with Katrina, and I knew the youth pastor and I weren't tight. Evidently, Katrina had asked for me when she woke up.

I went to the hospital, said hi to her, talked to her dad in the hallway for a while about his days in the Army, and then went to the waiting room where I played pool until my mother was ready to leave. It may seem corny, but something changed for me that day. I found myself thinking about her quite a bit. I remember even catching myself imagining us in a relationship. It definitely annoyed me, and I would never have admitted it publicly.

It wasn't too long after that I called her. I was nervous about venturing into any kind of relationship with her. We came from different worlds. If our families were ice cream flavors, mine would have been rocky road and hers would have been vanilla.

You could walk into the Martin home and tell not much had ever come into their lives that would upset the apple cart. Everything was in place. I had never seen a house with absolutely no clutter. It was like walking into a *Parade of Homes* house for the guided tour. Dave and Shirley Martin were well respected in the church. They were marriage counselors and he was an usher. They had three beautiful daughters. I'm sure they had little family issues, but it wasn't easily apparent.

On the other hand, my family was loud and our house cluttered. Furthermore, I knew I didn't fit the profile of a future husband for Katrina. Not that I was thinking about marriage, but having seen my own father in action, I knew fathers tend to look at boyfriends with a keen eye on the future, even if the boyfriend doesn't. According to my sister, her parents were looking to marry Katrina off to a pastor. I was no pastor in the making. Furthermore, I had heard from my sister that Mrs. Martin thought I had "devil eyes." Not exactly a ringing endorsement.

We talked a few times on the phone before I broached the subject of dating. Katrina told me that in order to date, I would have to have a "sit down" with her dad. That sounded reasonable enough. I'd seen my own dad give boys the third degree when they asked to date my sisters, so I figured that was part of the deal. I pulled her father aside one morning before church, and we had our "sit down." He explained his rules and I agreed.

One of the rules was that we could not date by ourselves. We were required to find suitable partners and have them approved by Katrina's father. Initially, because I was so eager to spend time with Katrina, I didn't think double dating would be so bad. But it wasn't long before I began to realize the limitations of such an arrangement. Besides, it felt strange to sit next to my date rather than across from her every time we went out to dinner. I can't remember one of those double-dates going well. Most times, we ditched our "partners" or they ditched us, depending on who was driving that night. Other times, the date would turn into a gender competition between the guys and girls. It was awful.

Our relationship was a disaster from the word go. I wanted more than she was willing to give. In my time with Denise, I had been the student and she had been the teacher. Now the roles were reversed. I wanted to teach Katrina all I knew, and I wanted her to be a willing student. The purity and innocence that attracted me to Katrina in the first place became a frustrating obstacle. She must have been exhausted, having to fend me off constantly. We fought constantly. One night, I got sick of the whole thing and went out with a girl from work whom I knew would "put out" and satisfy me. I wanted to make Katrina jealous, but she ended up breaking up with me. It looked like it was over.

Deep down, I really wanted to continue dating her. I was attracted to Katrina because, as I got to know her better, I discovered an authenticity about her. She was more than the plastic image I had in my head. She was the most optimistic person I'd ever met. She had certain "Pollyanna-ish" qualities about her that were like rays of sunshine. She was naïve, but I began to look at that as a positive. I'd dated girls with too much street knowledge for me, and her purity was definitely something I liked. Besides all that, I thought she was the most beautiful girl I'd ever laid eyes on. She was definitely worth another shot.

We had another sit-down. This time, it was both of her parents and me. I vaguely remember saying all the right things to get back in their good graces. Everything was going much better than I had anticipated, so I decided to drop the big one on them. I looked Dave square in the eye and said, "I love your daughter." I definitely had no idea at that time what love was. I just knew I had deeper feelings for his daughter than I had ever had about anyone else. He had a blank expression but said nothing to make me think I'd just crossed the Rubicon with him.

After I left, he told Katrina to break up with me for good. She was too young to fall in love, especially with me. The next night, she told me what her father had said. I was furious. I drove her home as fast as I could. I wanted to go in and have it out with Mr. Martin, but she begged me to stay out in the car.

I couldn't believe he'd played me for such a fool. I had talked to him the night before, and he'd said nothing about breaking up. In fact, he'd given his blessing to our continued dating provided we would abide by his rules. I would have accepted his judgment the night before. I was angry. I told Katrina that if she wasn't the sheep I suspected she was, she'd fight for me. She had told me that she loved me too, so why was I the only one swimming against the current?

In my mind, this situation was similar to my experience with Denise. I had encountered resistance from my parents too, and I had stood up to it. Of course, it had come at a high cost, but I hadn't yet calculated that. All I knew was that when I had a chance to fight for somebody, I'd done it. I had given up my home, my family, and basketball to be with her. I threw the idea in Katrina's face that she now had her chance to take a real stand on something, not one of those artificial deals within the safe confines of Emmanuel Baptist Church. No sir, this would be the real deal. I left her to think about it that night.

Reaping What You Sow

Two days later, we eloped to Knoxville, Tennessee. She had made her choice, and it was me. It was the first time I ever remembered anyone taking a public stand on my behalf. It would not be the last time she did it, either. I was sitting in Sunday School when an usher told me I had a phone call. It was Katrina. She was very calm. She said something to the effect of, "We'll never get to be together unless we get married. Come get me." My response has been the source of many laughs. I told her, "Don't do anything rash." I then sped out of the parking lot like an idiot and drove to her house.

She had everything packed and ready to go. Her parents thought she was sick, so they had gone on to church without her. We loaded up my old Buick Skylark as quickly as we could and then high-tailed it over to my house. Meanwhile, her parents became suspicious when they didn't see me in church. On a hunch, they decided to drive home and do some checking. They couldn't have been more than ten minutes behind us. She had left a note for them on the kitchen counter.

We went to my house and began packing up my stuff as fast as we could. My sister had stayed home with the flu, and she couldn't believe what she was seeing. I vaguely remember her trying to talk us out of it. We finished loading the car and hit the road. My sister told me later that her parents arrived about five minutes later.

No one could have told them what direction we were going because we didn't know ourselves. We must have looked ridiculous, though, in that tiny car, loaded to the gills, dragging the back bumper down the interstate. I had twenty-five dollars in my wallet.

Our plan was to go south and marry. We had a couple problems, though. One was that we had no money. I had $450.00 in a savings account, but it was in Toledo. This was before cash machines existed, so I knew I'd have to find a branch office of my bank somewhere along the highway in order to get my money. We left on a Sunday, so we wouldn't be able to get any money until the next day.

We were taking quite a chance leaving Toledo because we didn't know where we'd find my bank once we got on the road. As it turned out, in order to get away from her parents, we drove from Toledo to Cincinnati that day. We found a $20.00 hotel room and hunkered down for the night.

The next day, we drove back toward Toledo, hoping all the way to find my bank, but we didn't. We had to drive all the way back to Toledo to get the money. We hadn't eaten in two days, so the first thing we did after we got the money was to stop at an Arby's and eat like two starved dogs.

The second problem was Katrina's age. She had just turned seventeen. In fact, she was only a junior in high school. I was only eighteen, but that seemed positively ancient compared to her. We mistakenly thought that the farther south we'd go, the more likely someone would marry us in spite of the age problem. I had the prejudice that southerners marry anyone old enough to say, "I do."

We discovered that marriage without her parents' permission was out of the question. No one would marry us. So we came up with a new idea. We would write out our vows, go to a church, and read them to each other on the doorstep of the entrance. It would be beautiful, and a church wedding, after all.

Katrina was adamant that we had to have a real wedding, at least, a real one in our minds. She had fought me off for three months while we dated and again the night we stayed in Cincinnati. She was not going to consummate the marriage until we did it right, well, as right as we could under the circumstances. I didn't care what hoop I had to jump through or what the technicality was. I had one thing in mind, and I'd have done just about anything by that point to see it through.

We "married" ourselves March 5, 1990, in Knoxville, Tennessee. Because we had absolutely no money, we were living day-to-day in a hotel room. We contacted her parents to let them know we were okay, and unbelievably, they never demanded to see a marriage license. They believed our lie and sent us some money to get started. We both went out looking for jobs. Our honeymoon was a trip to Taco Bell topped off with a whirl in the bumper boats.

It didn't take us long to realize that one or both of us needed to go to college. After a succession of dead-end jobs, I arranged a basketball tryout at Cedarville College back in Ohio. Katrina's sister and brother-in-law who lived near Cedarville graciously gave us a room in their house to stay in until we got settled, so we moved back north after three months in Knoxville. I made the team when school started, and Katrina found us a great apartment near campus. Katrina took her graduate equivalency exam and passed it the first time. We received enough financial aid to get us through that first year.

Katrina worked like a mule as a full-time nanny that year. During my sophomore year, she tried to be a full-time student and a full-time nanny. Of course, she didn't last long under that kind of strain. Something had to give. She eventually gave up school and her nanny job to become a full-time waitress at Perkins Restaurants.

Sometime during our first year in Cedarville, the truth about our sham wedding came out. Not too many people found out, but enough. We were careful to make sure her parents were never the wiser. Technically, as I found out later, I could have been charged with kidnapping because she was a minor and I was an adult when we had crossed state lines.

My parents did find out, however, and immediately drove down to Cedarville. They paid for us to see the Justice of the Peace and make our marriage official. I had been holding it over Katrina's head every time we'd fight. I'd say, "We're not even really married. We could just end this today." I was using our lack of commitment as leverage. But my parents rightly demanded I act like a man and be a husband to my wife. Of course, as time would prove later, I really had no idea what being a husband was all about.

We struggled those two years in Cedarville. We had very few friends, and money was always tight. Katrina worked hard at her job. I worked at the college post office and the recreation center in addition to being a full-time student and a basketball player.

I grew increasingly frustrated at Cedarville. It was one of those "Christian" environments I dreaded. I thought I could play the game and get through, but all my old demons had come to the surface. I had problems with authority figures, so I had difficulties with my coaches and even some of my teachers. Cedarville required that all students fill out a church report to prove your church attendance each Sunday and Wednesday night. I thought it was none of their business, so I ignored the church report. I was always in trouble for that.

I showed disrespect for my coaches. It's amazing they kept me around as long as they did. I talked back and showed disrespectful body language to them. I walked off the floor in the middle of a junior varsity game because I was mad that my coach kept yelling at me from the sidelines. I went to the locker room and sat there for the rest of the game. One of the particular coaches was younger than I was and had never played. I had a hard time taking any coaching advice from him.

I fought with other students. One time, I hit a kid during a pick-up game in the recreation center, breaking his nose and cheekbone. I did it intentionally and felt no remorse. The funny thing was that he was a teammate and as close to a friend as I had on the team. I was suspended from school three days for that little misdeed.

The big problem in my mind, though, was that I didn't get the playing time I thought I deserved. I was used to being "the man" like I was at Whiteford. I was not "the man" at Cedarville, and I hated it. I would work harder and harder but get nowhere because I had no concept of team or being coachable. Consequently, I would take one step forward and two back.

All in all, we were reaping what we had sown. I had demanded Katrina make a decision. She'd made her choice to be with me against the wishes of her parents. I had taken her away from her parents without their blessing. There were going to be consequences for such behavior.

Katrina had grown up like most little girls, dreaming of a big church wedding with the white dress and the flowers. Instead, she got a Justice of the Peace at the Mayor's office in downtown Xenia, Ohio, in front of two witnesses. She never got her senior year of high school like I did.

Because I'd never dealt with any of my past issues, I brought a lot of baggage into our marriage. I had no idea how to be a husband. I was still very angry inside and lost my temper on a regular basis. Everyone had been so upset when I'd hit my teammate that day in the recreation center, and I couldn't understand their reaction because I lived with that anger every day. In fact, it was the same anger I had felt as a teenager. It had never gone away. It was always simmering just below the surface, waiting for a trigger mechanism to light it up like a roman candle.

Together, we bypassed pre-marital counseling, which could have headed a lot of these problems off at the start. Instead, we jumped into something sacred with no preparation for what lay ahead. College was not a fun time for us like it was for those around us. We were dealing with adult issues, but we were kids. I had constructed my entire personality upon the basis that I would not be bullied or cajoled into anything. I rejected sound advice because I wouldn't listen.

This may have seemed cool or trendy as a teenager, but, as a married man making adult decisions, it didn't fly anymore. I thought we could make a go of it all by ourselves. We didn't need anybody. The way I lived as a teenager, alone, angry, suspicious, distrustful, cynical, and fearful, became the way we lived as a married couple. We were reaping the whirlwind.

The next year, we moved to the city of Mobile, Alabama, for my junior year of college. We followed a coach who had left Cedarville for a similar coaching position at the University of Mobile. The school offered me a full scholarship to play ball, and that was all we needed to hear. It was hot down there, but there were lots of gorgeous beaches, the water was beautiful, and we soaked it up. The school paid for our apartment, and Katrina got a great nanny job with a nice family. Things seemed to be looking up.

It was the first time we became part of a church together. Dauphin Way Baptist Church was huge. A lot of folks called it "Fort God" because it sat ominously large right next to Interstate 65. We became active in a class for engaged and newly married couples called the "nearly-newlyweds" and everything was peachy. Well, sort of.

From the Lowest Valley to the Highest Peak

Our marriage was not in good shape. I ignored my responsibilities as a husband because I was chasing my basketball dream. I wanted to play pro ball overseas and make the big money. My wife was just along for the ride.

We were spending most of our time away from each other. I would get up each morning at four, and Katrina would take me to school where I'd work out until breakfast. Katrina had to be at work by six, and because the commute was long, it was necessary for us to keep this schedule. She would pick me up that night after study table at nine. We would go home, go to bed, and repeat the same schedule the next day.

There was another problem that existed between us. In fact, it was the fundamental issue. My wife was a believer and I wasn't. We were "unequally yoked" and it affected everything. It was like she was oil, and I was water. We couldn't mix properly because we came from two completely different perspectives. If the truth be told, we were both miserable.

It wasn't long before I made some stupid decisions. I got mixed up with one of the assistant coaches on the women's team and ended up having an affair. My commitment to my marriage had never been very strong. I liked the perks of marriage, but I wasn't about to work at it. The collegiate athletic culture of which I was a part did not lend itself to married students, either. The male and female athletes lived in separate dorms from the "regular" students, spent considerable time together on the road, and generally played footloose and fancy-free with relationships. There was a lot of innuendo and suggestive behavior that was exciting to behold.

I had grown dissatisfied with my wife because I kept mentally comparing her to the women I was surrounded with at school. They seemed so vibrant, beautiful, and full of life. It wasn't long before I'd rationalized in my mind that I could play with fire and not get burned. The affair lasted about six weeks. I knew what I was doing was wrong, but to be honest, I'd played around with this idea during our first three years of marriage. I was usually able to catch myself before it was too late.

The bottom line, though, was that in my mind, I'd already had affairs. This time, I wasn't strong enough to resist, and I crossed the line. Once I did, it was over. I lost my sense of shame and didn't care who knew. I flaunted it and dared Katrina to do something. I knew she'd find out eventually; I just thought I'd be able to explain my way out of it.

One night, I came home late after a road trip and found an empty apartment. Everything was gone. There was a letter on the counter, and that was that. I had no idea where she'd gone, but it was apparent that she knew everything. Katrina was in no mood for talking. The next day, I tried in vain to reach her but to no avail. All at once, I had several regrets. I guess the old saying about not knowing what you have until it's gone really is true.

She had called her parents, and they flew her back home. In a roundabout set of circumstances, she ended up in Atlanta, Georgia. The plan was to get her as far away from me as possible and for me not to know where she was. I had hit her on several occasions while we were fighting in the past, so her parents were concerned for her safety. It didn't help my cause when I found out she intended to divorce me. I went out and hit a lamppost in the Shoney's parking lot several times. I broke my hand with the first blow, and then I hit that post three more times. My fingers were pointing out the wrong side of my hand. There were many witnesses to that event, so when people heard I had been violent in the past, they put two and two together and agreed Katrina needed to stay as far away from me as possible.

I tried everything to win her back. I wrote letters. I sent gifts. I called her parents. I even went to counseling. I thought if I showed a token interest in all things "religious" she might be persuaded, so I showed a renewed interest in the church. The depths to which a man will sink to get his way are truly amazing.

She wasn't buying it, at least that's what I heard. I never knew for sure because I didn't know where she was. I knew she was keeping tabs on me through various sources, but I knew nothing about her. I've often wondered who read the letters and received the gifts I sent.

During this time my parents were amazing. They told me I needed to fight for the marriage. They believed marriage was for life, so they committed to helping save our marriage. They put their money where their mouth was. I racked up huge phone bills calling home because they were my lifeline.

Because I now had no money coming in, they would send me money to help out. But the stipulation always was that they'd support me as long as I focused on reconciliation. Both of my parents worked toward that end, and I'm grateful they did. Their compassion, at the time I needed it most, went a long way toward healing the relationship that had been broken for years.

Meanwhile, her parents weren't discouraging her plans to divorce me. Her father even offered to pay for it. I remember thinking that if marriage counselors weren't for the marriage, what chance did I have? I carried bitterness in my heart toward her parents for a long time after that.

It wasn't until I gave up trying to save the marriage that things began to happen. I went to my coach and gave up my scholarship. I told him I was dropping out of school at the end of the semester and returning home to Toledo, Ohio, to see if God would salvage my marriage. I still remember the glee in his eyes as he now had another scholarship to work with for next season. With my broken hand, things hadn't worked on the court as we had hoped, anyway.

I was absolutely heartbroken. Katrina and I had been separated for two months by this time, and our counselor had arranged a face-to-face meeting between the two of us. I had hoped this meeting would be a breakthrough. Instead, she informed me that the time apart had helped confirm her decision to divorce me. She was moving on with her life. I was crushed. That's when I went out, got in my car, and began the long trip north. I cried for most of the trip. I was at the end of myself.

I had been reading the Bible on my own during this time. Mainly, I started studying because I wanted to find out for myself what the scriptures said about marriage and divorce. I was looking for talking points to use against Katrina and her parents if I ever got the opportunity.

Through this Bible study, the Lord began opening my eyes to a certain reality. All of my relationships were a mess. I realized one day that perhaps my relationships here on earth were so broken because I had no relationship with my heavenly Father. Part of me, though, didn't want a relationship with a heavenly Father whom I believed, because of my memories of Grace Bible Church, was a grinch waiting to put the smack down on me for any little misstep. I imagined him sitting up in heaven with a giant people-swatter.

In spite of my hesitancy, I knew Katrina and I were finished unless a higher power intervened. As I was driving through Cincinnati, Ohio, I pulled over to the side of the interstate and said a simple prayer. I asked the Lord to forgive me of all my sins and to save me. I cried and told God exactly how I felt. I remember asking God to put back together the pieces of my life.

I didn't get a chance to continue because a state trooper pulled up behind me and flashed his lights. He came up and asked me some questions. I think he could tell I was having a tough time because he was very compassionate. I pulled back onto the interstate, and a peace came over me that I had never experienced before. Not one circumstance had changed me for the better except I was now a born again Christian with hope!

For the rest of the trip, the Lord flooded my mind with unresolved issues I needed to deal with once and for all. When I got to my parents house, I began by writing letters, letters to anyone and everyone I could think of whom I had hurt in the past. I began going to people and asking forgiveness. I sat down with my father, and we went through a lot of issues together. Forgiveness was offered by both sides.

I went to see Katrina's relatives who lived in the area, and I even made a trip to see her parents. It went like this: if God prompted me with a name from my past, I resolved to make things right with that person. It was the most cleansing period of my life. Burdens lifted and once broken relationships began anew.

I got a job working construction and was able to earn some money to pay a few bills. I ended up losing that job later after nailing myself to the frame of a house with a nail gun.

My father paid for me to attend a Bible conference in Detroit with the Parsons. I went for four straight nights after work. In that conference, I received good teaching about marriage and learned some Biblical principles that would make a difference in my life.

God was doing a work in my life during those couple of months. I was not striving to reach Katrina. In fact, I felt such a peace that I was able to lay that burden down and not worry about it. Every now and then I'd pick the burden back up, but I now was equipped to recognize it and release it again.

Meanwhile, the Lord was doing a work on Katrina, too. She called me out of the blue one day after four months of separation and informed me she was coming to Toledo to visit her parents. She told me that she would be attending church that Sunday, but she did not want me to make any attempt to talk to her. She then went so far as to tell me of her intention to go to the same Sunday School class I had been attending. Again, she repeated, "Make no effort to talk to me. I just called you to let you know."

I listened to all of that and finally could hold back no longer. I asked her, "What kind of game are you playing? I have no problem staying away from you, but it seems a little strange for a married couple to be sitting there acting as if they're single and expecting everyone else to feel the same. It's going to be a little awkward, don't you think?"

The conversation got heated, and I ended up hanging up on her. Afterwards, I couldn't believe it. I wanted more than anything to be reconciled with this woman, and I just yelled at her and hung up the phone on her. I shook my head at myself.

I'll never forget that Sunday morning service. I have no idea what the message was about. I couldn't tell you who preached. We sang songs I'm sure, but I don't remember. I just sat there in a fog. I kept thinking that this was as close as I had been to my wife in four months. I felt the Spirit's presence in that service more than ever before.

At the conclusion of the service, before the customary four or five verses of "Just As I Am" could be completed, I saw Katrina running down the aisle. I was stunned. She made it to the pastor, and they hugged. I thought that was odd because I still had our phone conversation ringing in my head. The pastor stopped the music and informed the whole church that Katrina had come forward to reconcile her marriage. People were crying everywhere. I sat down, stunned.

It seemed like her entire family had shown up together for this service. Many of her relatives had come to show support for her. I believed it was an act of defiance, but it didn't really matter. They were stunned. Her father left the service and sat in his car. I suppose I would, too, if my daughter married a melon and then went back to him. I'd probably have to go somewhere to sort out my thoughts. I mentioned earlier how she had stood up for me when we first got "married" and how she would do it again. Well, here she was, doing it again. Only this time, we were doing things God's way.

Pastor Fuller took us out to lunch at Red Lobster, and we sat next to each other. It was the most surreal lunch I ever had. I had so much to tell her, and I figured she could say the same. We decided to take it slow and work our way back gradually. She continued living at her parent's home and me at mine. We met each morning before I had to be at work and had devotions together.

By Friday of that week, we were both ready to be husband and wife again. We stopped at the side of the road that evening and prayed over our marriage. We asked God to be the center and to guide and direct us the rest of our lives. We asked for mercy and grace to help us in our inevitable times of need. We hugged and went on the honeymoon we had never had. It was only overnight, but it was special nonetheless. We were truly in love for the first time. I no longer felt anger, and I'm sure she could sense that. God had taken a teenage rebel and a lousy husband and turned what I had made ugly into something beautiful.

Unconditional Love

We moved into an apartment in Toledo in 1993 and resumed our life together. It was a strange time. We had just come through something traumatic and survived. We had been walking an emotional tight-wire. Feelings of anger, betrayal, hopelessness, grief, revenge, the list could go on. After we reconciled, the emotional balance swung to the other extreme. We were living in a fairy tale.

It wasn't long before Katrina was pregnant with our first child. We were so excited we both almost ate our way into a lifelong membership at the nearest IHOP. Shelby Elizabeth was born in February, 1994. I was so excited about being a dad that I even got up in the night a few times to feed her. I found that the excitement wore off quickly, though.

I found a job doing data entry for a chiropractic firm and soon realized I'd better go back to school. About that time, I received a phone call from Coach Scott Williams. He was my coach at Cedarville and Mobile. He had taken a new job at Pillsbury College in Owatonna, Minnesota. After the small talk, he asked me if I still wanted to play ball. I had one year of eligibility left, and his phone call definitely started me thinking. I persuaded Katrina to go, and we rushed off to the Land of 10,000 Lakes.

Pillsbury wasn't exactly our cup of tea, but we reasoned

it would only be for one year. It was like going back in time. The legalism reminded me of my past. I could have recited from memory the list of dos and don'ts that made up the Pillsbury student handbook. All the old prohibitions were there. The Gestapo-like snoops were all over town, waiting to catch people.

We lived off campus so we could get away from the eyes a little. I was required to take several Bible classes, and it didn't take long to establish myself on campus as someone they'd need to keep tabs on because my ideas about the Christian's role in this world might pollute the others. One professor told our class that *Promise Keepers* was "of the devil" because it incorporated people of different denominational backgrounds. I shook my head and rolled my eyes at that. Before long, I discovered it was pointless to argue, so I took a newspaper with me to class and read the sports page. I'm sure that confirmed my status as an infidel.

There were some bright spots, though. I loved playing ball again. We had a decent team, and I was named to the second team, small college All-American team at the end of the year. As for life outside basketball, when things got too slow around campus, we would load up and go to the Mall of America in Minneapolis.

After the 1994–1995 season ended, I had free time, so I got a job at the local Wal-Mart. My wife had been working as a waitress and on weekends as a sitter for mentally challenged people. I had begun entertaining notions of playing professional ball overseas. I made some calls and found an agent to represent me. He filled my head with crazy notions, one of them being that if I signed a contract, I would need to go alone. The way he explained it seemed to make sense. However, basketball was coming between my family and me again.

And then, it happened. I had another affair. It happened quickly. The first time, the relationship meandered around and developed slowly. Not this time. The second affair lasted much longer than the first. The first was purely physical, but this time I could feel myself becoming emotionally involved.

Meanwhile, my agent called and said I needed to move closer to his base of operations in Columbus, Ohio, so we packed up and moved back to Toledo. I thought I had walked away from this affair like I did the other one, but soon after we moved, I began calling her and trying to figure out ways to see her. I was becoming irritable around Katrina. She asked me what was wrong on many occasions. I told her it was the stress of waiting to find out about my basketball future when, in reality, it was guilt.

One night in the car, we began fighting and, at a loss for words, I spilled the beans. Katrina was in shock. I've never seen her so hurt. She literally shut down for weeks after that. She refused to leave her bedroom and wouldn't eat. I couldn't reach her, which was probably good because she wouldn't have believed a word I said anyway.

The turning point came during a walk we took together. We were walking in the country, and we had it out. Katrina didn't normally like confrontation, but this time she let me have it. She was angry. Her face turned red, and she screamed at me. She beat with her fists against my chest. She said our marriage was over and I would *never* deceive her again. I just stood there and took it. What else could I do?

God intervened right there. For the first time, I saw what

my actions had done to her. After the first affair, I came home and she was gone. This was different. The consequences of my actions were staring me in the face. I was quiet for what seemed like a long time before I said, "I'm sorry." It sounds preposterous now, but she looked me in the eyes and said, "I know." She grabbed my hand and we walked home. She no longer felt lifeless and cold. In fact, she responded to my touch. I didn't know what just happened.

That night, she told me that she had promised God when she came back the first time that the decision was final. She had made a vow. She said that she had made a decision to love me again when she came back. It was not a decision based on emotions. She was staying with me because she had made a promise to God. In fact, she even gave me permission to continue my lifestyle if I so desired, but she wasn't going anywhere.

I have never forgotten the look in her eyes as she demonstrated unconditional love that night. I didn't deserve another chance. I knew that. I only know that she had passed her test, and I had failed mine.

However, if any good came from it, I was keenly aware that Katrina's response to me and my failures didn't look or feel like the kind of religion I'd grown up with. I would have been shunned or banished.

I had watched as Christians around me had picked out the faults in everyone and everything until there was nobody left. They thought they were being set apart, when, in reality, they were the Pharisees with whom Jesus had numerous run-ins. The Biblical account of the Pharisee standing on the street corner for all to see and thanking God that he was not a sinner like all the people around him could not say it any better. By the world's standards, Katrina had every right to wash her hands of me and say what that Pharisee had said. But just as Jesus, who didn't come to condemn but rather to save, she chose not to condemn me.

Of course, that didn't keep me from condemning myself. One of the byproducts of legalism is the self-loathing it promotes. Nobody can keep all the commandments. Legalism inevitably turns its finger of accusation back on you. I had never measured up in my own mind. I had used it as a crutch, but with God's and Katrina's forgiveness and acceptance, I knew my crutch was gone. I had begun to journey along a new path, one without the condemnation of legalism.

I began praying from that moment on for God's protection. Since it was obvious I had the backbone of a wet spaghetti noodle, I knew I needed God to be my wall of protection. I was beginning to learn about spiritual warfare the hard way. I began asking God each day for him to place a "hedge of thorns" around me and my home.

Later, I talked with a trusted friend about it. He pointed me to two stories in the Bible. David fell to the temptation of Bathsheba because he lingered on it after he saw it. Joseph, on the other hand, stood up to the temptation of Potiphar's wife by fleeing the scene. He explained it like this, "See and Flee." It made sense, and I've used this little principle ever since. We decided the basketball dream was finished. It was time to grow up and finish what we had started. I enrolled at the University of Toledo in the fall of 1995 and set out to finish my degree.

PART II

Where is Cheatham County?

For the next two years, we struggled to finish my college education at the University of Toledo. Somehow, I had managed to cram four years of school into seven, and finally, in the spring of 1997, I graduated with a degree in secondary history education. I had also worked during that time as an assistant basketball coach at Whiteford under my mentor, Coach Rice.

Upon graduation, I made a promise to Katrina. She had worked just about every kind of rum-dum job one can imagine to get me through school. I told her I'd take the first job offered to me. She asked if she could send out a couple of my resumes to places she picked out. I said yes, never dreaming of the consequences of that little conversation.

Now that my dream of playing basketball was in the past, I had replaced it with the dream of being a coach. So naturally, I sent about seventy-five resumes to the states of Indiana, Illinois, Ohio, and Michigan. My wife, on the other hand, sent two or three to Tennessee. I've often asked her what possessed her to pick Tennessee, and she's given me different answers. God was leading in the job search because by sheer volume, it stands to reason that we'd end up in the Midwest somewhere, but he had other plans.

I received a call from Cheatham County, Tennessee, within

one week. We loaded up the car and headed south. I thought I'd go through the motions of an interview but never would I take a teaching and coaching position south of the Mason-Dixon Line. I wasn't even sure they played basketball in the south. Unfortunately, the interview went great. Cheatham County's secondary supervisor gave me the third degree and was sufficiently impressed (or fooled) to offer me a position on the spot. What could I do? I had made a promise.

They needed coaches, so the high school principal roped me into coaching girls' volleyball in the fall and boys' soccer in the spring. I knew absolutely nothing about either sport. In fact, if truth be told, I hated soccer. Nothing that occurred that spring changed my feelings toward that activity, either. The varsity boys' basketball coach hired me as his freshman coach, so I was going to be a busy man.

That year was a blur. In the fall of 1997, my wife gave birth to our second child, Toby Gavin. Our family had doubled in size, and according to a southerner's way of thinking, I was now the proud papa of a car and a truck! My teaching mentor at the high school told me that since I was in the south, I should start thinking like a southerner. Girls were cars, and boys were trucks, four-wheel drive trucks with a gun rack, a rebel flag, and of course, it had to have a custom horn that played "Dixie."

Between the ninety-minute commute, the normal teaching load, and the coaching responsibilities, I was gone before sunrise and home after sunset. I saw my family on weekends.

Katrina was busy with two small children, and we were in an unfamiliar place. We were already making plans to leave Cheatham County at the end of the year when God intervened again. I had been offered several different jobs. One was an assistant basketball coach's position in Clarksville near where we lived. I would have been close to work, the pay would be better, I would be working for a head coach I respected, and the school was loaded with talent. It seemed like a no-brainer.

Other opportunities existed as well. In the past, I probably would have jumped first and asked questions later. But this time, we began praying about our future. I even went to my pastor and consulted with him. Brother Verlon Moore was the senior pastor at Hilldale Baptist Church. Within five minutes of our first visit to Hilldale soon after moving to Tennessee, I knew it was the right place for us. I had a lot of respect for Brother Moore, and I loved his personality. He was a no-nonsense straight shooter, no games, just the truth. I could relate to someone like that. He gave me some good advice that day, and I decided not to take the job in Clarksville.

Meanwhile, Cheatham County had grown so much that the school board had decided to open a new high school in the northern part of the county. I knew nothing about this until the actual staff hiring began. One day, Tim Ray, a teacher with whom I'd eaten lunch on occasion, approached me and indicated that he was going to be the athletic director and assistant principal at the new school, Sycamore High School.

He asked me if I'd be interested in coaching girls' basketball. I first said yes, but then reconsidered. I figured that would be the end of it. He came back a week later and asked me to consider the boys' head coaching position. He added that there were about four other candidates ahead of me, but I should keep it in mind anyway. Again, I thought I'd never hear from him again. A week or so later, he said there was only one candidate ahead of me. I started to wonder what was wrong with the situation for three people to say no.

The longer I live, the more I'm convinced God has a sense of humor. People had been asking me what I thought of the opportunity to be Sycamore's first coach. I had told everyone who would listen that I considered it a dead-end proposition.

I had heard that the school was going to take two classes and build a high school from them. In other words, they would start with eighth and ninth graders and add a grade each subsequent year. It sounded very nice, unless you were a coach.

Because schools have a window of opportunity during which they can become full-fledged varsity members of the Tennessee Secondary School Athletic Association (TSSAA), Sycamore had to make a decision. If it joined during the first opportunity, SHS would have varsity sports earlier, but they probably wouldn't be competitive.

However, if it waited until it had its first senior class, those first couple of classes wouldn't have varsity sports until their senior year. It would be a mass exodus. Sycamore chose to join early. This meant the first few teams would be butchered on a nightly basis. It looked like an impossible situation from my perspective.

I should have seen it coming. The job I had turned down in Clarksville made sense. It was the smart thing to do. This Sycamore thing was a pipe dream. It was impossible! My mind kept screaming at me not to be a fool. But my heart, what should I say to my heart? I reasoned that surely God would close the door, and that would be that.

A week later, he called and offered me the job. I didn't know whether to be excited or not. I wasn't the first, second, third, or even fourth choice, so I'm sure Mr. Ray wasn't that excited. A part of me thought that God was punishing me because I had told people that whoever took the job would be a sacrificial lamb. *He would be expected to start a program from scratch, struggle through the early years, lose a bunch of games, and then get fired for all his efforts.* Those words of mine kept ringing in my ears. I just knew my Father was sitting on his throne with that big people-swatter, and I had just been too fat and juicy a target to pass up.

As far as timing goes, I wasn't entirely convinced Sycamore was the right fit for us, but we had prayed about it and felt a peace with the move. I respected Mr. Ray and his judgment, so in the spring of 1998, we accepted the position with much fear and trepidation.

We moved from Clarksville to Pleasant View and set up shop at Sycamore High School. There was a lot of excitement in those first couple of years as the new school got off the ground. The community support was tremendous.

My wife got a job driving a school bus, so, in a real sense, we were on this journey together. She became the bus driver for the basketball teams, and for the first time, basketball was something we did together. The county installed child-safety seats in the front seat of her bus, so we were able to make these trips as a family. It was a special time.

We had started the year at Cheatham County Central High School and spent the majority of the year planning our move back north. We'd been tempted by a seemingly good opportunity, one which seemingly would have been the logical choice, but God steered us into a future that seemed much too big an undertaking for us. Just like putting the pieces of our marriage back together would have been an impossibility, God was getting ready to show us his power again.

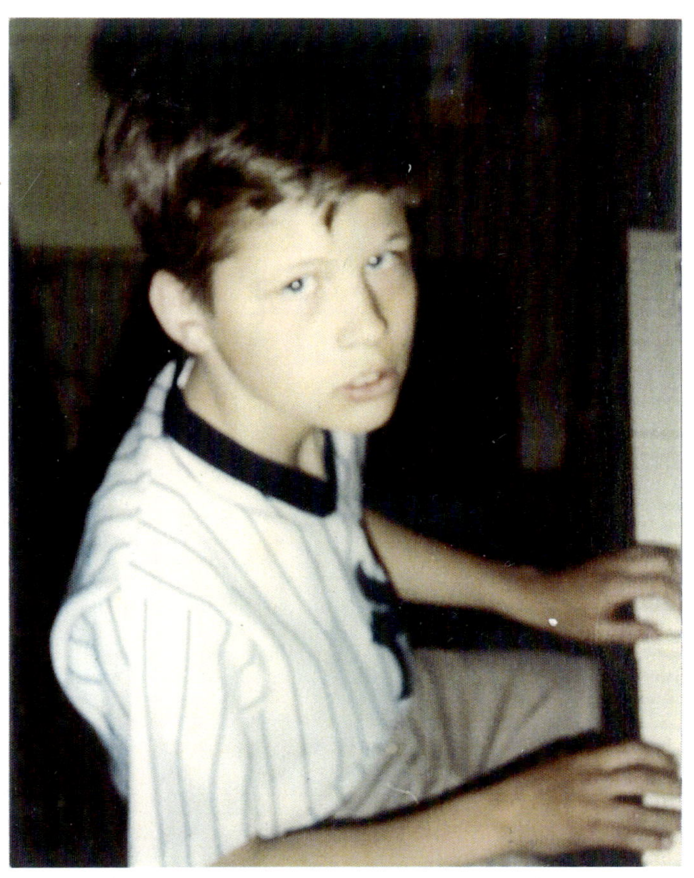

The facial expression says it all, doesn't it?

My first exposure to the game of basketball...our hapless little team at Grace Baptist Academy.

My senior year playing for Whiteford High School and Coach John Rice.

First prom night.

Katrina and I at our wedding shower,
after the fact, of course.

Katrina and I during my senior year in college.

Katrina and I shortly before our separation.

Shelby Elizabeth, our firstborn, hamming it up at a Sycamore homecoming.

Toby Gavin, our oldest son, loving the action at Chuck-e-Cheese!

Casey Marie, daughter number two, with all the spirit and spunk of her daddy!

Sammy Nathan, our youngest, always smiling!

Sammy's "growths" beneath his left ear and beneath his chin during the dark days of Obion County.

Bobcat Jones hot

By BILL BRENTON
Evening News sports editor

OTTAWA LAKE — Whether he's from Fort Wayne or Angola doesn't matter. Whiteford's Barry "Indiana" Jones played Friday night like one of Bobby Knight's Hoosier collegians.

The 6-4 transfer from the Angola area scored 42 points, pulled off 12 rebounds, blocked 2 shots, dished out 2 assists and had a steal while carrying the Bobcats to a 79-76 victory over Morenci before a packed house of screaming fans.

The senior center who doubles as a deadly 3-point shooter didn't pick on some patsy, either. Morenci came to town with a 12-3 overall record and a game behind Whiteford in the Tri-County Conference race.

Larry Bruce's Bulldogs left southwestern Monroe County with their fourth loss, only a slim chance for a TCC title share and not-so-fond memories of the brilliant Jones.

"It's the best game anyone had against us all year," the veteran Morenci coach said. "We're used to doing that to other people. Jones hurt us, though, and we were all over him."

Jones was Mr. Everything after the Bobcats fell behind 20-6 in the first quarter, gradually rallied when Coach John Rice changed defenses and held off a late Bulldog burst.

It was great entertainment for a standing-room-only turnout estimated at 850 persons by Whiteford Athletic Director John Flynn.

"Barry has gained confidence as the season went along. He now thinks his potential is unlimited," Rice said with a smile which revealed he didn't care a bit about that.

Aggressive with every rebound, going strong to the basket every time he got the ball inside, shooting 3-pointers with no hesitation and thrusting his fist in the air after every field goal, Jones also was far from bashful in talking with reporters afterward.

"I wanted this one for Coach Rice. I felt I let the team down before (12 points in a 66-62 loss at Morenci)."

Jones played at Grace Baptist as a freshman in Angola and for Angola High School as a sophomore. He was out of basketball last season but is making up for the lapse like a parched man at a water hole.

"I'd always been a guard and had a bad habit of forcing things at first. I thought I had to do it all when I came here. I thought I had to be the main man.

"Now I've adjusted to coach's system. Scoobie (Chris DuPree) still is the main man."

It would have been difficult to convince partisan followers of either team of that fact Friday night, however.

The 185-pounder whose personal goal is for a college basketball scholarship answered every Morenci burst with a salvo of his own.

He scored three straight field goals to reduce the early Bulldog margin, then five consecutive baskets to allow Whiteford to trail only 44-43 at halftime and finally six in a row during a third quarter which shoved the Bobcats in front to stay.

Included were four of his team's seven 3-point buckets. DuPree had the other three at crucial times.

Rice provided the perfect example of a now-complete Indiana Jones averaging 31 points and 12 rebounds a game the last 7 times out.

"We were only 2 points ahead and they were pushing us with just 50 seconds left," the 16-year coach said. 'It's Crunch Time,' Barry spoke up. 'I'm ready to go.' "

"Earlier in the year I wouldn't have wanted the ball. But I do now," Jones said after Friday's game.

Slick substitute Jake Kornbluth found the lanky Hoosier inside for a 3-point play which wrapped things up.

Ranked sixth among Michigan Class D schools by The Associated Press, Whiteford is certain of at least a share of its third consecutive league crown. The Bobcats are 11-1 in the circuit. Whitmore Lake and neighborhood-rival Summerfield remain. The fast-breaking team stands 15-2 for all games.

"It was a typical Morenci-Whiteford game," said Bruce with more than a trace of pride for a gutty showing. All five Bulldog starters reached double figures in scoring.

Brad Stevens' Whiteford reserves set the scene with a 59-52 preliminary win. Scott Longanbach (20) and Mike Foldvary (11) set the pace for victory No. 10 in 17 starts for the young Bobcats.

BIG NIGHT — It was Indiana Jones making the Whiteford High School Gymnasium a Temple of Doom for invading Morenci Friday night. Jones is using his left hand to score 2 of the 42 points he amassed in a key win over the Bulldogs. Morenci players are Todd Sutherland (14), Lonnie Tompkins (32) and Kirk Bruce (right).

One of my favorite high school memories was this game. (used with permission)

Indiana Jones finds home at Whiteford

By RON MONTRI
Evening News sports writer

OTTAWA LAKE — The first thing Barry Jones does is take a snow shovel and clean the court.

Then he puts on gloves to keep the hands warm. Can't shoot with stiff fingers.

Then he tests the wind to see how much he will have to alter his shots to compensate for the breeze.

It isn't easy playing basketball outside in the winter, but Jones has his own concrete court at home. He has spent a great deal of time on it in the last year trying to become a better basketball player.

He has succeeded.

The same player who was the last boy on the bench a few years ago has become an All-Stater on today's Associated Press Class D team.

Indiana Jones — as he was nicknamed after transferring from Indiana — averaged 24.7 points and 11.4 rebounds a game this season in helping Whiteford to a 19-3 record and a Tri-County Conference championship.

The son of Mark and Sue Jones of Ottawa Lake has been to schools all over Indiana, Ohio and Michigan the last four years. One of the luckiest breaks of his life came the day his father landed a job at Owens-Illinois in Toledo. The family eventually bought a house in the Whiteford school district no more than a long jump shot from the Michigan-Ohio line.

A hundred yards to the south and he would have gone to Sylvania Northview, but he wound up at Whiteford and it is the best thing that has happened to his basketball career.

It brought him under the wing of a disciplined, knowledgeable basketball coach named John Rice.

"I didn't know how to come off picks. I didn't know how to take a defensive stance," Jones said. "He's taught me more in one year than everybody else put together."

He has been learning about the game since the eighth grade when he was at Syracuse Christian School in Indiana. It was so small there was no athletic program.

Jones transferred to Grace Baptist High School, but there were no signs he was on the road to stardom.

"I was only 5-7 or 5-8 then. I was shorter than my mom and gangly. I was the last kid on the bench and sort of a folk hero. If Barry scored, it was a big thing," Jones said.

He wanted to become a solid basketball player, but it doesn't happen overnight.

"I decided I was going to work real hard that summer. I went down to the park and they stole the ball from me left and right. I got the ball stuffed in my face all the time," he recalled.

It was discouraging until he saw Larry Bird in a television interview. "I never had any money when I was a kid. I never had anything. I just worked my butt off for basketball," Bird said.

Barry decided he wanted to do the same thing. He practiced more often. He painted lines on the court at home, shoveled snow off it and even used salt to help melt the snow and ice. He began to grow in ability and size.

His father is 6-8 and weighs 230 pounds. "So I knew my size was going to come," said Barry, who still is growing at 6-4 and weighs 185.

He averaged 22 points a game as a freshman and 24 as a sophomore. But the competition he faced at Grace Baptist wasn't the best.

"I wanted to get a college basketball scholarship and knew I couldn't do it there," Barry recalled.

He transferred to Paririe Heights, then Angola, then Toledo Emmanuel Baptist and finally Whiteford. He found a home with the Bobcats and Rice, a straight shooter who lets a kid know where he stands.

"I've forgotten more basketball than you've ever learned," Rice growled at one early practice.

The words hurt, but Jones knew the coach was right.

"I did what I wanted at the other schools. I was content to stay out there (20 feet from the basket) and be lazy," he said.

There also was a major adjustment in officiating.

"It's a much more physical game in Indiana. Michigan calls fouls real tight," Jones said. "I'd get two fouls right away and then lay back. He'd take me out because I wasn't playing any defense."

The last straw came at Whitmore Lake when Rice blistered his team with a halftime tirade. "He said if anybody shot anything outside of a 10-footer they were coming out and he was looking right at me when he said it," Jones said.

Indiana Jones posted up inside, and a star was born.

He scored 24 points in the second half and 37 for the game. It started a point parade unmatched in Region history.

Jones averaged 12.3 points a game in the first 4 contests of the season. He averaged 31.5 in the last 10 games after moving inside. Included were nights of 44 and 42. He finished the season with 543 points, breaking the Whiteford record of 530 set by 1988 All-Stater Brad Nieman.

He has gone from a timid player to an All-Stater. The one-time bench-warmer now has confidence in his ability. Some basketball followers might describe him as cocky.

But Larry Bird is his hero. Always has been and probably always will be.

"Larry always says you have to have confidence in your ability," Jones said. "I heard him tell a story once about having a dream that he was playing one-on-one with God and won. I'm not ready to say anything like that."

When the reporter asked me where I'd like to go to do this interview, I told him I needed to take him to the place I felt most comfortable—my backyard basketball court. (used with permission)

My last year playing competitively.

Former Whiteford rebel has life in order

By RON MONTRI
Evening News sports editor

OTTAWA LAKE — There were tears in Barry Jones' eyes.

His wife, Katrina, also was crying.

When Barry flipped the tassel to the other side of his cap Dec. 14 and officially became a college graduate, only he and his wife fully understood all the struggles they had endured to earn that diploma.

It took seven years. Jones took classes at five different colleges from Alabama to Minnesota.

His educational odyssey mirrors his life. Jones attended six high schools in three states before graduating from Whiteford in 1989.

He has traveled an even longer and more winding road with his life and his marriage, but he and Katrina believe their best days are ahead.

Looking for a feel-good story during the Christmas season? Try this one.

It's about a boy who was 15 when his parents, tried of his rabble-rousing, asked him to leave home. He was taken to a type of reform school but escaped by hiding from the police in a doghouse.

Barry was 18 when he and Katrina eloped to Tennessee with $20 in his pocket.

Jones is the first to admit he was a rebel and a troublemaker. But don't judge him on his past. He is a different man now at the age of 25.

Wednesday he sat near the Christmas tree at his parents' home with Katrina and their cute-as-a-button daughter, Shelby.

Barry has patched things up with his parents, Mark and Sue Jones. His once-shaky marriage is on firm ground. He has a college degree, will start a teaching career at Bedford Jan. 6 and is an assistant basketball coach at Whiteford.

He appears to have found the peace and maturity that was missing much of his life.

He'd like to thank his parents for sticking by him the last few years. He'd like to thank Whiteford coach John Rice for giving him some direction. Most of all, he'd like to thank Katrina for seeing the potential for goodness in him that others missed.

During his high school career, people looked at Barry Jones and saw a gifted athlete, but a defiant youngster. An All-State basketball player, but a troubled boy. Katrina saw something else.

"When we were dating in high school, he was rebellious, but I guess I thought I could save him," she recalled.

This was before "Touched by an Angel" became a television hit, but Katrina could have played the part of Monica trying to save a lost soul. Except she was married to the man she was trying to save. And their marriage was on the rocks. Katrina even left him for several months.

"That's when I realized how much I loved her," Barry said.

Katrina wasn't as anxious to patch things up.

"We were separated four months. But when we got back together, I looked him in the eye and saw something had changed," Katrina recalled. "There was a maturity that hadn't been there before. We talked like we had never talked before."

To prove his love, Barry vowed to give up college basketball. He had been spending four or five hours a day with the game and it was one of the problems in the marriage.

He quit basketball — and college — then returned to school when the marriage stabilized.

Jones had been attending the University of Mobile in Alabama. He resurfaced at Pillsbury College in Minnesota and blossomed into a star. After scoring 117 points in a three-game tournament in Chicago — a 39.0 average — and setting a school record with 21 rebounds in a game, Jones earned second-team All-America honors.

He thought he had a chance to play basketball in Europe, but that fell through. They returned to Michigan and Barry completed his college courses at Toledo.

— Evening News photo by Lyndon Steele

Whiteford assistant basketball coach Barry Jones (left) once was something of a rebel but now has his life in order with the help of wife Katrina and daughter Shelby.

He became an unpaid volunteer coach at Whiteford last season, rejoining the man who had a profound impact on his life.

"John Rice taught me everything about basketball. When I came to Whiteford (as a player), I didn't even know what a backdoor cut was," Jones recalled.

Rice taught him other things, too. He wasn't afraid to discipline the rebel.

"He threw me off the team after one game," Jones said. "We patched things up on the bus ride back from Morenci. He had the guts to stand up to me and call a spade a spade. I admired that."

Now that Jones has resolved his childhood anger and channeled his ambitions in a positive direction, Katrina sees some qualities in him that she admires.

"He stands for what he believes in. He's never been one to go with the flow," she said. "He has an incredible drive to persevere. He got his degree after all those years and it was one of the happiest days of our life. I cried when he put his tassel to the other side. So did he."

Now they have a career to look forward to. And they have Shelby, who is 2½. This was the first Christmas where she was old enough to be filled with wonder and awe.

Those who know her father might be filled with the same awe after seeing him make such a personality transformation.

"He's a great father. He puts her above himself," Katrina said. "The Lord has pulled us through some real struggles, but I know He has a special plan for Barry."

The same reporter who wrote many of the stories about me in high school interviewed Katrina and I during my senior year in college for this follow-up. (used with permission)

My first coaching gig—helping Coach Rice again at Whiteford.

My first varsity team as head coach at Sycamore, at Larry Bird's high school gym in French Lick, Indiana.

I took my first varsity team at Sycamore to team camp at Indiana University. Here we are after playing on Assembly Hall's floor after yet another beatdown!

My best team at Sycamore after winning our first district championship!

Some of my all-time favorite kids—three seniors who willed us to victory against some pretty overwhelming obstacles.

Coaching demands passion!

Sal starting for Sycamore High School as an eighth grader.

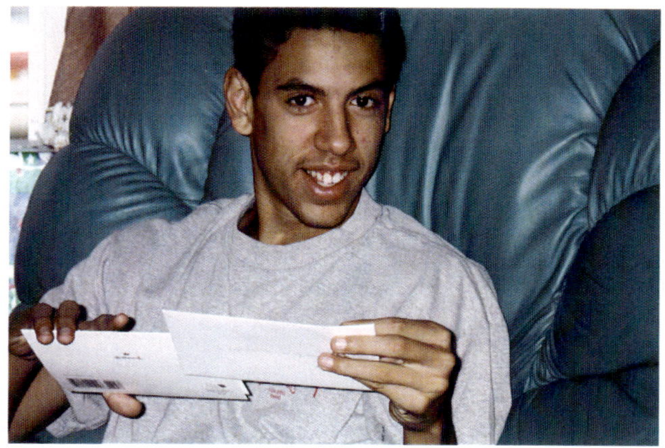

One of my favorite memories of Sal was the last Christmas he spent with my family.

The Jones family—summer 2007 on our back porch in Campbell County, Tennessee, overlooking the beautiful Cumberland Mountains.

Leadership 101

When Sycamore opened its doors, I think we all anticipated a rough beginning. I'm not sure, however, that we could ever have fully realized the difficulty ahead of us. The year before, an eighth grade boy had collapsed and died on the basketball court during practice. He had died in front of his teammates. Those were the same players I was now inheriting as our first freshman class. Needless to say, there was fear.

Two weeks into our first basketball season, the girls were practicing and an eighth grade girl collapsed and lay unconscious on the court. The girls' coach and I administered emergency breathing for what seemed like an eternity. It was no use. Katie died while we waited for the ambulance. Two deaths in less than one year on the same court and under the same circumstances.

In the hysteria that ensued, there were many people who thought our gym was cursed. They said the county should tear it down and build a new one. Some thought the whole school was contaminated from something left over during its construction. They said the ventilation system was spreading this contamination and killing their kids.

For a while, some folks even blamed the coaches. Both incidents had happened during practice. Sycamore was still a middle school the year Adam died. His coach had been running conditioning drills when he collapsed. Adam had asthma and had gone over to the scorers table to use his inhaler but didn't make it. I heard that the conditioning had been too hard for the kids, and that was what killed him. That theory was later debunked by the autopsy, but for a while, it lingered. In Katie's case, practice had just started. No one had even worked up a sweat. Again, her autopsy revealed a defect in her heart. She could have died sitting in a desk in a classroom.

Nevertheless, there was a cloud hanging over the basketball program as we tried to get it off the ground that first year. On more than one occasion, parents objected to my conditioning methods. I had not been directly involved in either situation, but both my players and their parents had. I could understand their fears.

I also had a job to do. I ended up losing two kids we had high hopes for because of everything that had happened. As time went on, it became less and less of an issue, but for a while I wondered if basketball was going to make it at Sycamore.

We did manage to make it through the first year, though. Since we had only eighth and ninth graders, we played a freshman and junior varsity schedule. We all knew what lay ahead. We were going to be playing a full varsity schedule the following year, with freshman and sophomores no less.

The second season was brutal. We lost in every imaginable way there was to lose. One five-day period, we lost four games by a combined total of 195 points. Try explaining to your players that they're getting better after mind-numbing totals like that. I thought I might not make it.

Because the school board had not drawn up school zones,

we were forced to recruit our athletes. We had to give the ones we had a reason to stay. We knew there was little chance of us picking up kids from other schools because no one wants to go somewhere and lose. It was difficult to coach under those conditions. Playing with a short hand was bad enough. The net result was instability. Players came and went. Parents used the situation as leverage against the coaches. My assistants and I just kept working. We poured blood, sweat, and tears into those kids often for naught.

Other obstacles included the lack of resources. Cheatham County did not support any of its athletic programs with a budget. By necessity, coaches had to be fund-raisers. In those early years, the needs were pressing. We started a booster club and raised thousands of dollars for a weight room, a sound system, and lots of equipment. We started a junior basketball league for kids and raised thousands more to buy uniforms and other gear for the players.

We had another roadblock I hadn't even considered. For years, Cheatham County had been known as a "coaches' graveyard" for boys' basketball coaches. A coach would come in and try to put his imprint on the program and invariably, a parent would take offense and run to the powers that be. Rather than support the coach, these powers would push the coach on down the road. A new coach would come in, and the cycle would repeat itself. There were a few parents in the community with well-deserved reputations as "coach slayers."

I had no idea, but several of my first players belonged to these kinds of parents. Since I was not from Cheatham County, I was not familiar with the lay of the land. I was blind to the politics. My boss, however, had seen it all before.

Tim Ray had lived in Cheatham County his entire life. As luck would have it, he had been the boys' basketball coach for a few years at Cheatham County Central High School. He'd been successful, too. His teams won several district regular-season or tournament championships and produced several collegiate players including one professional. For Cheatham County, that was quite a feat.

However, he had also coached several of the older brothers of the players I now had on my team. In other words, he'd dealt with the same parents. He had given up coaching after a point because these forces wore him down, and he got sick of it. He had not gotten the kind of support from his bosses that any coach needs to help stand up to the pressure. He stepped down more out of aggravation with them than with the parents.

With this backdrop, I went to work every day having no idea of the forces conspiring against me. Early on, when we were losing and I was making most of my mistakes as a coach, parents did what they'd always done in Cheatham County: they beat a path to Tim's door. His experience, though, had taught him to stand up for his coaches. He had told me on more than one occasion to "make it possible for him to defend me." As long as I didn't box him into a corner, he'd stand his ground.

He could see these parents coming a mile away, so most of the time he could prevent something from occurring before it actually happened. I thank God for steering me into my first coaching job where I could learn through much trial and error, but with a strong support system from my boss. I was fortunate. Many coaches who are better than me have had opposite experiences.

The first varsity season was a test of survival. We finished with a 2–25 overall record. We took a lot of beatings, but my kids never laid down. We measured success by comparing scores of our first game against an opponent to the second game. We tried to win quarters, or, if that was too optimistic, just four minute stretches. As a coach, I learned to use every time out to stop the bleeding when teams were making their big runs on us. At the end of the year, I was proud of my fellas. There was no pressure to win, just to show improvement.

We had accomplished that, and so we were pleased. The second varsity season, however, was one of the most trying experiences I've ever had. With the last year fresh on my mind, I was determined to show improvement. I felt internal pressure to win, and I passed that on to the players. I pushed and pushed.

As a coaching staff, we felt there was some dead weight we needed to eliminate. The only way I knew to get rid of players who weren't committed was to work them to death. So physical conditioning was brutal and practices were long. I fell into the doom-loop that many young coaches do when they're young and trying to make their mark: work harder, longer, and with more intensity. And while you're at it, take all the joy out of it. In college, I had learned in economics class that more is not necessarily better. It's called the law of diminishing returns. I should have applied that principle to my team.

We did improve on the court. Our final record was 12–18, and we made it past the district tournament and into the regional. The year had left a sour taste in my mouth, though. There was dissension among the troops from start to finish.

Players quit in the middle of games, players stopped speaking to one another, and parents screamed at me in the parking lot after games. I cracked after one of our close losses, chasing the officials off the court and into their locker room. I had to take stock of my leadership and honestly come to the conclusion that it was poor. It was a tough pill to swallow.

I decided to do something about it. Hilldale Baptist Church was offering a class in leadership. The book they were using was one of John Maxwell's. Maxwell taught me that everything in life rises and falls with leadership. If an organization has good leadership, it will be reflected in the people. If it has poor leadership, that too will be reflected in the people. To blame the people for lack of purpose is to indict the leader. I also learned that leadership really is all about influence. My players would only "buy in" to me as their leader if I had influence with them. Influence could only be effectively wielded if it was genuine. He drew the distinction between leadership and power. Many of the things we talked about in that class really applied to my situation.

Maxwell gave practical examples of his own personal growth process. One of his examples jumped up and grabbed me around the throat. He told of how he had sent out letters when he was a young pastor to ten or so other people in leadership positions and asked for one hour of their time in exchange for $100.00. The interviews gave him a deeper insight into leadership and greatly benefited his ministry.

I decided that imitation would be my sincerest form of flattery. I made a list and sent out the letters.

The responses changed my life. One coach sent me his book. I read it from cover to cover. Another referred me to a web site. Two others agreed to face-to-face interviews. During one such interview, we didn't even talk basketball. I told him about our team chemistry issues and how basketball didn't seem fun anymore. He gave me advice only an experienced coach could give. I took extensive notes. He even sent me home with one of his team notebooks to help me become better organized.

All in all, that off-season was the most productive I'd ever had. I'd been to camps and clinics and learned strategy and tactics, but that spring taught me how to lead with the heart and show compassion and empathy. That seemed to be a recurring theme in my life. I didn't understand how to show compassion or demonstrate empathy. My relationship skills just weren't good.

I thought about things and concluded that I'd never seen compassion or empathy in practice around me. My background had influenced me to such a degree that even though I hated what it stood for, my past kept dictating my present and future. I kept reproducing the lessons I'd consciously or subconsciously learned at Grace Bible with my team, my family, my social circles, and my work. I didn't like it, but it was what it was.

That class taught me that the fun would return if I made it less about me and more about the kids. It may seem simple, but that was a revelation for me.

I decided to put these principles into practice. I could still be tough. I just needed more balance, a little compassion here, a little understanding there. I threw our code of conduct out and reduced our team rules to one: don't do anything to embarrass yourself, your team, or your family. It was pretty broad, but I was no longer boxing us all into a corner and being lazy with my leadership. It dawned on me later that my precious code of conduct was nothing more than a list of dos and don'ts like I'd grown up with at Grace Bible Church.

In our fourth year at Sycamore, I knew I would be coaching my first group of seniors. They were good kids. I decided to pass the lion's share of the leadership role down to them. I would pour myself into them, and they, in turn, would lead their teammates.

The results were astounding. The seniors took over ownership of their team and led on the court and off. Games we used to lose in the fourth quarter due to a lack of on court leadership, we were now winning because the players could lead themselves. I did less that year than ever. I rewarded the team with days off and easier practices.

We still went hard, but not as long. We focused more on the positive, and instead of taking advantage of the situation, the team responded and worked harder. It had a snowball effect. Basketball was fun again, and best of all, I was developing relationships with my players. It was no longer an adversarial relationship. We were all in this together. *Together* became our motto.

I decided to try this approach at home with my own kids. I remembered how I feared my own father, and it occurred to me that I had the potential to be the same way. So I began to change. I also applied this newfound wisdom to my relationship with my assistant coaches. It was amazing. Every relationship I had improved dramatically.

The Lord used basketball to teach me about leadership. He used it to get my attention and change me for the better. Just like he used fishing analogies when talking to the disciples, he met me where I was. I probably wouldn't have learned it any other way.

We finished that season with a 23–11 overall record. We advanced to the round of sixteen (sub-state) and scored some dramatic upsets along the way in the tournament. It was a fun year.

A lot was happening at home, too.

Not My Will, But Thine

In September of 2000, my wife gave birth to child number three, Casey Marie. I'll never forget her birthday because I had planned to go to the Notre Dame versus Nebraska football game that fall in South Bend. It was promising to be a big game, and Katrina's due date was two weeks before. If everything went as planned, I could be present for both events.

However, Casey didn't cooperate. The due date came and went. As game day approached and Katrina was still *very* pregnant, I knew I'd better take my assistant coaches up on their generous offer to take the tickets off my hands, thus preserving my relationship with my wife. They were convincing as they sincerely reminded me of my priorities. Sure enough, just as Nebraska scored the winning touchdown in overtime that day, Casey was born. A man never forgets an event such as that.

People were beginning to notice our family. I think they thought Katrina and I didn't realize what caused children to happen. We started hearing the comments. We had a houseful, but I had grown up in a family of seven. It was not unusual to me.

Hilldale Baptist Church had proven to be a tremendous source of encouragement and a place of growth in the life of our family. Katrina had begun teaching a ladies' Bible study and was having a blast. It was also during this year in particular that one of the pastors had taken me under his wing.

Brother Howard Fuller and I had met the previous year, and we struck up a friendship immediately. He was not your typical pastor. He was down-to-earth and encouraging. In fact, no single person has had more influence with me and my spiritual journey than Brother Howard. I even asked him to be our team chaplain. I think he enjoyed that role very much. He would come speak to the guys. Sometimes they'd ask him questions or just shoot the breeze with him. He even ate a worm once in order to illustrate his point during one of his talks. The players really liked him. Anyway, he had facilitated the John Maxwell leadership class I joined at church. I guess he saw something in me during that class and decided to get me off the sidelines and plugged in.

He started a new Sunday School class and had me fill in for him on days he couldn't be there. I started noticing over time that I was filling in more and more. One day, he called and said the class was mine. I told my wife I'd ruin the class. I had zero confidence and felt unqualified to stand in front of adults teaching the Bible.

The dear folks in that class embraced Katrina and me, and before long, I was having the best time I'd ever had in church. We developed friendships, and our little class grew. It was a tremendous blessing. I started noticing how much I was learning by teaching. God was stretching me and expanding my horizons. It seemed that every week, the lesson hit me square between the eyes.

One week, the lesson was about obedience. The gist of

it was the following: Are you prepared to say yes to the next step of obedience God has for you? When God reveals the "what," will you trust him for the "how"? I taught that lesson and wondered what shoe the Lord was getting ready to drop on my head. I found out the following Tuesday.

We got home late that night from an away game at Waverly, Tennessee. There was a message on the answering machine. I retrieved the message and called the number. It was Sal. I had coached Salvador back when he was in eighth grade. He had been to seventeen schools by the time I met him.

He was quiet and withdrawn. He never had a ride home, so I was his transportation. When I'd drop him off at home late in the evenings, I began to notice the dark, empty house. He never had any money on our road trips. Sal was basically going through life on autopilot. He'd changed schools so many times he didn't want to make friends because he knew he'd have to leave again anyway. He was always alone. Basically, from what I could tell, Sal was raising himself.

Furthermore, he was racially mixed. That may not be a big deal in most places, but in Cheatham County, Tennessee, it's still a big deal to some. He told me once that he felt all alone because he was the only black kid in our school. When I asked him if he'd feel better in a city school, he surprised me and said no. I didn't understand. He said that blacks wouldn't accept him because they didn't consider him to be black. In other words, he didn't fit in either place and he knew it.

He had left Sycamore during his ninth grade year, and I'd lost track of him. This was the first time I'd talked to him since he'd been gone. In a nutshell, Sal needed help. He asked me if he could come live with my family. He had been arrested for stealing a car with his girlfriend and had no place to live. I called his mother to get the rest of the story.

He'd been skipping school and was fired from his job for stealing. His grades were a mess, and he was headed down the same path as both of his older brothers. One was incarcerated in a federal prison for breaking and entering, and the other was in state custody for reasons I've never been too clear on. His mother said she felt like she'd "lost him" and was desperate for our help. She said she'd give us legal guardianship and let us parent him the way we parent our own children.

Before the phone conversation ended, I knew what we had to do. I looked at Katrina, who had been listening to the conversation, and she began nodding and urging me to take him in even before I'd hung up the phone.

I remembered our Sunday School lesson and decided we would take him in. There were legal problems to deal with. Once they were sorted out and we had legal guardianship, my assistant coach and I took a truck, loaded up his belongings, and moved him into our tiny basement. We spent the rest of that school year trying to get him academically straightened out. His transcripts were a mess, so that was quite an undertaking. He practiced with the team but mainly filled the role of student manager that year as he earned his way back into the fold.

Incidentally, Tim Ray and I had a conversation before the basketball season even began, and I had told him this was going to be my last year. We were going to leave Sycamore at the end of the year. Again, God had other plans. I knew the last thing we could do to Sal was leave and go somewhere else. The Lord does indeed work in mysterious ways. I went back to Tim and asked him if I could swallow my earlier words. He was very gracious about the whole thing.

Too Easy

At the end of our fourth year at Sycamore, we had three varsity seasons under our belt. Things were looking up. The leadership that had developed the previous year had produced a new class of leaders for the next. We returned a lot of experience for the upcoming 2002–2003 season. That experience paid off as we finished that season 28–6, won our first district championship, and advanced to the sub-state again. We finished as runner-up in the region to the eventual state champion. It was a good year.

Sal's grades were looking up, and his behavior had been pretty good. We'd had some turbulent times when he first came to us midway through the previous year, but it seemed he'd adjusted after all. He started for us at point guard and played well. He lacked confidence, but that was to be understood. I figured another year would do him good. I really believed if he kept working hard, he could possibly parlay his talent on the court into a college scholarship. I began planting that seed, hoping to spark something inside him.

Katrina was busy driving the bus and caring for three kids and a husband. We both continued teaching at Hilldale and grew in the Lord. The year seemed to be characterized by peace and harmony on every front, a welcome change after some of the previous years.

Relationships were blooming everywhere. The Lord had birthed new friendships through our Sunday School class and Katrina's ladies' Bible study. Never in my life had I encountered the type of deep, meaningful relationships that we did through Hilldale Baptist Church.

Way back at the beginning of our Sycamore experience, one of the smartest moves I made was to hire Shelby Tinch as my assistant coach. He had been an assistant for Tim Ray. When I was hired at Sycamore, Tim recommended him. Because I trusted Tim, I asked Shelby to join my staff without knowing him that well. It was the first decision I made as a coach, and probably the best.

Shelby was an elementary physical education teacher in the county. He had lived in Cheatham County his whole life and knew everybody. His job gave him additional insight to the kids we would be coaching because he'd had them all in his class at one time or another. He proved to be a terrific coach. He helped me in more ways I could ever list. But, the true measure of him was not his coaching ability. Shelby was a man of his word. He told me the first day I met him that he'd be loyal to me and to the program. He promised not to hold back and be a "yes man."

As it turned out, he did exactly as he promised. I never once worried about my assistant coach stabbing me in the back. Nervous ninnies learned to stay away from Shelby because he didn't want to hear their nonsense. He'd defend what I was doing. If he couldn't defend it, he'd just walk away. In keeping with his second promise, if he couldn't defend something I was doing, he would have already told me.

Since relationships are built on trust, I grew to rely

on Shelby. We became friends as well as work associates. Many times, he did things behind the scenes to help my family. He always seemed to sense when I needed to hear an encouraging word.

Our friendship eventually spilled over to include my other assistant. Vic Shelton had come along during our second year. He too was a good friend and a great coach. The relationships I formed with these two men blessed my life. We had many good times together traveling on scouting ventures, going to basketball clinics, and most importantly, eating out. Coach Tinch loved to eat.

Eventually, Shelby transferred from the elementary school to the high school. He wanted to be closer to the program and in the building with the kids he was coaching. I always appreciated the sacrifice he made to start over in the high school. He even went back to school in the summer to get certified to teach drivers' education.

At the beginning of our third year together, he took in two foreign exchange students who ended up playing for us. It was always funny to hear his latest story about Besian and Moritz. As a single guy, Shelby was pretty set in his ways. Moritz kept eating all the ice cream and leaving the refrigerator door open. Neither one knew how to make a new jug of sweet tea after they had finished the last batch. Shelby would come in to the office just shaking his head. He couldn't believe Moritz had just eaten an entire package of cookies. It was hilarious.

That was the year I realized that I had carried a lot of bitterness in my heart toward Katrina's parents. I had a long list of grievances. It had become a wedge issue in our home.

Over time, I sensed a different perspective beginning to take root. Maybe it was having kids of my own. I don't know what to attribute it to except that the Lord was working on me.

I actually grew to appreciate their approach to parenting. After all, hadn't it produced one terrific wife? That was only one example, but there were many others where God turned my thought process 180 degrees. And so, on our annual trip up north to visit family over the holidays, I stopped along the way and had a brief chat with them. I told them about where I had been, where I was, and Lord willing, where I wanted to be in the future. I asked their forgiveness and they gave it. Our relationship has blossomed ever since.

As it would turn out, it was a year of rest, a year to gear up for an impending train wreck. Our sixth year at Sycamore and the three subsequent years proved to be the toughest years I had ever gone through, professionally and personally. I later thought that I must have really stepped in it because God was squishing me like a bug.

What Goes Around, Comes Around

We began the 2003–2004 school year knowing lots of change was in the air. My daughter Shelby would be graduating from elementary school at the end of the year. Sal would be graduating from high school, and Katrina had just given birth to our fourth child, Sammy Nathan. Before the school year began, I began to pray earnestly that God would bless and favor us as a family, that he would enlarge our territory, be with us, and keep us from evil. I began praying these specific words every day as a result of reading a little book by Bruce Wilkinson called *The Prayer of Jabez.* I must confess that there have been moments since when I've wondered why on earth I ever prayed such a prayer.

God began to work in ways that could only be described as mysterious. First, he led us away from our beloved church family. It was one of the hardest decisions we had ever made as a couple, especially because we had no reasons to tell people. It confused everyone, including us. One thing I had learned, though, is that when God says move, you had better move. So we left Hilldale.

Secondly, the school year started, and we began having trouble with Sal. It was little things at first. The problems at home spilled over into the classroom. Then they virtually wrecked our team. He had turned eighteen over the summer, and I'd given him use of the car. This newfound freedom did to him what it did to me when I was a kid. He went wild. I tried to give him rope, and he kept hanging himself with it.

He got involved with people who weren't helping his cause. He began participating in their vices, and before long, I wasn't able to reach him anymore. He became insolent and uncoachable. Teachers were having problems with his behavior, and the administration was getting involved. He was close to accomplishing so many of his dreams, but also close to throwing it all away.

During this time, I basically lost the ability to communicate with him. He started refusing to come home. Instead, he'd stay out with his friends. I'd try to track him down at school, but you can only pull a kid out of class so many times. Tim Ray spent hours with him in his office trying to connect. When he did come home, a nervous edge would come over all of us. He wouldn't even look me in the eye.

He wrecked the car one night. Rather than tell me, he called and said he was quitting school to join the navy. My wife took the message. I tracked him down and found out the truth, or at least what I thought was the truth. After we got past the navy ruse, I found out about the car. He told me what had happened, and I told him it was okay. "It's just a car," I said. We hugged and I thought we'd made a break-through.

I found out later the story he told me had been a lie. In fact, I began catching him in quite a few lies. Rather than taking time out to think, I just kept reacting to Sal's behavior. If I'd taken a moment and thought about it, I might have seen the parallels between his life and mine. I might even have spared myself the pain that was to come. Perhaps I could have altered my approach a bit.

I now realize that life had indeed come full circle. I was my dad, and Sal was me. When that realization sank in, I wanted to do what Waylon Jennings so poetically said a man should do if he's in love with the wrong woman: "Dig a hole, crawl down in, and pull the ground right in over you."

He'd been cutting quite a few classes. I started checking on him like I would a child. I was frustrated that he couldn't understand his behavior was completely unacceptable. I was sick of his excuses about his past and his family. I felt like he used any crutch he could to evade the consequences when he got in trouble. One day, I caught him in the cafeteria when he was supposed to be in class. When I confronted him, he looked at me, smirked, and said, "I'm out of class; you're out of class. What's the difference?" That's when my powder keg blew.

I told him to meet me in the locker room. When we entered, there were several team members inside eating lunch and watching TV. I told them to leave and locked the door behind them. Sal was standing there, slouched over, looking at me with that same smirk. I walked up to him, grabbed him, and threw him to the floor. I jumped on top of him, grabbed his head in my hands, and made sure I had his undivided attention.

By this time, I was pretty worked up. He was crying and telling me he was sorry. I'd heard all that garbage before. I held him there while some graphic communication took place. When I'd finally run out of things to say, I got up and that was that. He just sat there. I told him the ball was in his court now, but one way or another, if he wanted to stay in my home, things were getting ready to change. I walked out and wondered, *what have I done?*

He did what most kids would have done. He went to all the highways and bi-ways looking for sympathy. It wasn't long before the whole school knew what had happened, or at least his version of what had happened. I had to explain to my seniors what had taken place, and, of course, the administration needed to know.

I'll never be able to thank Tim Ray and Dr. Chester enough for standing behind me on that one. The way they looked at it was that it was a family matter. It was unfortunate that it happened on school property, but the overriding factor was that I was Sal's legal guardian. I had disciplined him for behavior that they were well aware of.

That probably helped. Everybody knew Sal's history. Everybody was aware I was having problems with him. When you get right down to it, everybody was having problems with him, so it was no mystery.

On Tim's advice, I called his mother and explained everything. She actually thought the whole affair was good for Sal. She said something to the effect of, "He's never had a man in the house before. I'm glad he had the fear of God put in him by somebody."

After the dust settled, I knew Sal's time with us was over. Sal's pride was not going to allow him to come back into my home and put himself under my authority after that. It was just a matter of time.

He didn't come home that night or the next. I think he believed I'd just let him drift through the rest of his senior year with no accountability. He wanted to move in with a friend, but I told him no. Way back at the beginning, when we were in the custody proceeding, the judge had told me in no uncertain terms that he expected me to carry this thing through to Sal's graduation. I was made accountable to help steer him through all of the legal obligations he had to fulfill after his arrest and to get him through school. I couldn't do that by letting him run wild.

I knew what I had to do. I also knew it would rip my heart out to do it. I sat down with my assistant and we talked it over. He agreed, so I cut Sal from the team. I then called his mother and told her to come get him. By cutting him, I'd lost any leverage I had with him at home, so cutting him from the team meant kicking him out of my home, too. It truly broke my heart.

Sal called me that night and we talked. He was contrite, and I wished him the best. I told him I'd help him in any way I could. We hung up, and I felt a dull pain throbbing throughout my entire body. I wanted to be sick. I had wanted to connect with Sal so badly, but when I thought about it, I knew I had made many of the same mistakes my parents had made with me. That realization took the wind out of my sails for a long time.

Sal had become a part of our family. He was good with the kids, and they loved him. He called my wife "Miss Katrina," and they had become very close. It was a tough time at the house, but that would prove to be the easy part.

The next day, I stood before the team and explained everything. Nobody was happy about the turn of events. The senior class was very close, as they'd been through a lot of wars together. This fractured relationship and loss of a key player left the whole team stunned. It reminded me of a boxer who staggers after absorbing a severe blow. We were definitely staggered. To make matters worse, Sal ended up across the county at our rival and was declared eligible by the Tennessee governing athletic body. In other words, Sal would be competing against us. It was indeed an ironic twist, one that felt like a twist of a knife.

This all happened one week before the season began. Sal was our all-region, all-district, starting point guard, and now he was gone, under traumatic circumstances no less. It left quite a hole. Needless to say, we started the season horribly. We lost close games at first. We had no confidence. I would look out on the court and wonder what had happened to the boys I remembered. We had no joy. We were playing with no heart, just through the motions.

I overreacted after one particular loss, and five kids walked out of practice and quit. Things were bad. All five eventually came back, but it would get worse before it got better. We traveled to Harpeth and only scored six points in the first half. We couldn't do anything right. Meanwhile, Sal was scoring and having a great time. It looked like you could stick a fork in us, because we were done. Christmas break couldn't come fast enough.

Thank You, Lord, But ...

Another of my enduring memories of the 2003–2004 season was how lonely I felt. Katrina couldn't drive the bus because she was caring for a newborn. I used to sit next to her while she drove, and we'd catch up after away games. Tim Ray was going through his own grief as he had lost his wife in a tragic car wreck, and Brother Howard had taken a new position as a pastor in Kentucky.

I usually spent a considerable amount of time talking with these three during the course of any year, but due to circumstances beyond anyone's control, they were not available. It was a lonely time. I learned to be still and talk to the Lord quietly instead.

Meanwhile, our search for a church home was a disaster. We tried here and there. Neither of us were excited about anything. Something was missing. I hated trying out new churches because everybody wanted to talk to us. They wanted us to fill out visitor cards, among other things.

Everybody knew us by virtue of the size of our community, but also because of my position. If we didn't return, feelings were hurt. I just hated the whole thing. We stopped searching and began having church at home. I actually grew to enjoy our little devotional times. Katrina and I both knew it was a temporary fix. We just couldn't seem to trace the path God had for us. We were in a perpetual state of restlessness.

After Christmas break, the team began to slowly gel. We still didn't win all of our games. We would win one and lose one. Then we'd win two, and lose one. It was slow and steady progress. I threw out everything we had been doing, and we went to a very simple offense.

We loosened up practice considerably and just worked on live competitive situations. Then we'd crank up the tunes and let the fellas shoot. If I had walked into one of these practices during my first couple years as a coach, I'd have thought it was nuts. Depending on your perspective, I had either slipped a cog or grown as a leader.

Our schedule was brutal. We'd intentionally scheduled very good teams in an effort to get us prepared to get over the sub-state hump we'd been straddling the last two years. At that time, we had four seniors returning and a group of younger kids who could play. It had seemed like the right thing to do.

But when our starting point guard was kicked off the team and we encountered other problems along the way, the schedule no longer seemed like such a good idea. We could get no relief. There were no easy outs on the schedule. However, as we improved and became competitive again, I could sense a little confidence returning. By the end of the year, we were springing upsets on teams who looked at our record and assumed we were a bunch of chumps.

We actually went into the district tournament with a losing record. But I knew we were a dangerous team because we were peaking at the right time. We also had several players with tournament experience, winners who understood how to turn it up a notch. Sure enough, we won game one and moved on to the district semi-finals against Sal's team. Harpeth had destroyed us at their place the first time. The second time, Sal had bailed them out in overtime, and they beat us on our home court.

Harpeth had been the best team in the district during the season. Nothing that happened during the first three quarters of this game seemed to indicate an upset was in the making. In fact, with six minutes left to play, Harpeth led us by thirteen points. Then, everything completely changed.

I've never been a part of a game like that. Randy True and the other seniors refused to lose. Momentum changed in a blink, and Harpeth's undershorts got tight. We ended up winning by six points. A nineteen point swing in six minutes! I look at that game the way I look at the time I was running through the streets of Fort Wayne and was caught. I don't know to this day how I got free, and I don't know how we won that game. I think God had something to do with it.

We went on to win our second straight district championship and advanced the next week to the regional finals for the third consecutive year. We ended up losing in the substate to the eventual state champion, and I was devastated. I knew I should be grateful for the way the season ended, but I felt God had let me down. I was disappointed with God.

Not By Might, Nor By Power, But By My Spirit

Before every season, I would spend time praying for my team and the upcoming year. I would pray for each player and coach by name and seek God's wisdom. The Lord always gave me a word for each team during this time. I remember God's word to me for each team I coached.

In the early Sycamore years, God spoke to me using the story of the Israelites' journey into the promised land. He promised to remove obstacles from their path "little by little." He was very clear about not doing it all at once because the result would leave the Israelites vulnerable to other dangers. I had been praying for the team, and the Lord led me to this passage. I, of course, was hoping for a quick fix, but God was promising he'd be with us on the long journey. This word never changed until I began praying for my first team with a senior class in 2001.

At that time, we were coming off the disaster of the 2000–2001 season, when we had all kinds of team chemistry issues. I had been taken to God's school on leadership. As a result, I probably prayed more about the 2001–2002 team than any other. God led me to a passage where he promised a new "season" of "peace and harmony; fruit and harvest." The Israelites were coming out of a dark period, and God wanted to give them hope. I don't know how they took it, but I was happy as a clam to see this new word for my team. This word carried us for the next two years.

My last team at Sycamore had been promising to be more personal than most, though I didn't know at the time that it was going to be our last year. I started praying about this team earlier than the others. As we were riding home on the charter bus after the season ending loss in the sub-state game, I began praying over the 2003–2004 team. I knew it had the potential to be a great team. Sal would be entering his senior year. We had a good group of seniors and a talented bunch of underclassmen. We would be good and everybody knew it.

I was a little frustrated by our inability to get past the sub-state level, and that was the focus of my prayer. "Lord, what can I do to get us over this hump?" I remember, like I would remember being struck by lightning, the response I got. Again, he directed me to the passage regarding the Israelites and their impending march into the promised land.

Out of fear and hesitancy, they sent spies ahead to search out the land. They brought back an ominous report. The people began doubting God and his promises because the people were "literally gigantic," and they lived in cities surrounded "by walls that reach to the sky." This report put fear in their hearts, and they missed out on God's best for them because they didn't trust.

I knew instantly what God was saying to me. God had a promised land for me and my family. If we knew the obstacles to that promised land, we'd never enter into the blessing he had for us. If we could see the giants facing us, we'd lie down and wallow in self-pity. If we could see the walls that reached to the sky, we'd never try to fulfill the destiny he had for us. He was asking me to begin a new journey, one with tremendous blessing and favor at the end. He was asking me to trust him and begin taking baby steps in that direction. That was the context surrounding my decision to read Wilkinson's book and begin praying the prayer of Jabez.

Of course, in that moment, I immediately applied the word I had received to my team. I had always been hesitant to claim big things in the past because I was afraid I'd look like a blooming idiot if I went public with something and it didn't happen. Nevertheless, my dream from day one had been to win the state championship. Equating my dream with the promised land, I decided to trust God and claim big things. I decided to be bold about it.

I went to Tim Ray and asked him to make our schedule for next year as hard as he could to prepare us. I added more summer camps to our off-season schedule, and we played more basketball that summer than we had in a long time.

I added a new component to our pre-season conditioning program. We already had a reputation for having one of the toughest pre-season programs. "Gut Week" had become a tradition. It was a ten-week program that prepared the guys for one final week of conditioning challenges. Each day was a different challenge. The final day was "graduation day." It represented the end of the pre-season and the beginning of basketball season. Each player had to run a full set of Green Bay sprints, a predetermined number of hills, a predetermined amount of conditioning drills in the gym, and finally, one mile under six minutes to graduate. As each player graduated, I'd give them all their gear. It became quite a rite of passage.

"Dawn Patrol," the new requirement, became our morning part of the conditioning program. We'd all meet at 6:00 a.m. and lift weights. We divided the team into groups, and each day a different group was responsible to bring breakfast for everybody. After we lifted and did a little shooting, we'd all gather for breakfast. The guys would then shower up and go to first period.

All of this was designed to win us a state championship. Unfortunately, we didn't. In fact, the season almost went down the toilet before we made it to Christmas break. I couldn't understand what went wrong. When the season was over and we had come up short again, I thought that either I didn't hear God right or he forgot about his promise. I think everybody must come to a point in their spiritual journey where they begin asking the tough questions. I was at that point.

Gradually, the Lord revealed to me what probably is easily apparent to anyone reading this. All he wanted was the glory. He promised the Israelites that he'd give them the promised land. They were to be obedient and follow him in. He certainly didn't need whatever strength and might they brought to the table to make it happen.

Good grief! I had fallen into the same trap. God had told me think bigger. He wanted to "expand my horizons" like he did with the Israelites. But he wanted to do it his way. I wanted to do it my way. I worked like a pack mule to make it happen.

I was trusting in my "warhorses," so God took one of them away. I was trusting in my methods, so God had to make them fruitless and counter-productive. Because I was stubborn, I almost ruined my team.

I wanted the promised land, but I wanted to earn it. I wanted to feel as though I deserved it if it did happen. God couldn't give it to me on those terms because he wanted the glory and I wouldn't let him have it. It's so apparent to me now that I was merely acting out my legalistic, works-oriented understanding of God. Again.

As I think back, I can see little warning signs I believe God was giving me along the way to warn me of impending disaster. I remember summer ball when we looked worn out. We were playing just to play. It was doing us no good at all. We ended up losing a series of games that week, and it put some doubt in our hearts.

As a coach, I should have seen that. I was too busy "making it happen," though, so it completely escaped me. Later, during our pre-season conditioning gauntlet, I should have seen the burn-out on the fellas faces. Rather than being fresh, they were sick of each other and basketball by the time we started the season.

Once the Lord was able to knock some sense into me, my outlook changed. In spite of me, God gave my team a wonderful gift from above. He did what he is good at. He took my trash and made it into a treasure. At one point in the season, we were 2–10 and last in our district. We finished the year 18–17 and first in our district. We ended up in the sweet sixteen for the third year in a row. That was the new perspective I had on our season. After all we'd been through, I was so proud of the fellas for hanging in there. I'll never forget the 2003–2004 senior class.

Some time after the season was over, Sal came over to the house for some chicken wings, and we were able to gain closure in that period of our life as a family. I'm thankful God intervened in that relationship and brought some healing. He invited us to his graduation at the end of the school year, and we went. Later on, his mother invited us to her home for his graduation party. Sometime during the aftermath of him leaving us, God gave us a peace about Sal. He's like the rest of us: in God's hands. We were just thankful to have played a small part in his life, like those who had done the same for me.

As the school year came to a close, we still had not found a church home. We weren't looking that hard. Meanwhile, the same stirring we had in our hearts to leave Hilldale had been moving in our hearts to leave Sycamore, too. For the first time, I began to consider the possibility that the word I had received, which I had applied to my team, was really a word for my family and me.

That was when I began to learn about God's timing and how different it is from man's timing. The promised land I was looking for couldn't be contained neatly within man's framework of a basketball season. I began to sense that it was much bigger than that, and that it would take much longer than I had originally hoped.

I resisted the stirring for a while. One day, I read from the book of Jonah. I noticed how his initial disobedience had far-reaching consequences for those around him. They hadn't done anything wrong, but they got caught up in something bigger. I thought about my boys on the team. It broke my heart to think of leaving them. I made every excuse I could think of. I tried making deals with God. But I kept thinking of those poor sailors on Jonah's boat. I knew if God was calling me away and I stayed, those same boys I was staying for would be the ones to suffer. With last season fresh in my memory, I decided to obey. I tendered my resignation at the end of the 2003–2004 school year, and we began packing up the house.

PART III

Sin in the Camp

At the beginning of the 2004 summer vacation, we moved our family up north to live with my parents while waiting for God's direction. Leaving a secure job behind and all the other things that came with our home was scary. But, according to Proverbs, our role was to trust God and acknowledge our complete and utter dependence on him. He told us not to lean on what we could see and understand. If we would just trust him, he promised to "direct our paths."

I said all these things and knew they were true, but it was very hard to live out at times. During that year of waiting, I battled all of the familiar tendencies. I felt pressure as I looked around me and saw four children and a wife. I looked at the things I could see, and nothing added up. No job, no home, no schools for the kids, no church, and the list went on. That's when I began toiling and spinning in my mind. When I took my eyes off him, I felt like I was going to go crazy waiting.

Five months into our northern exposure, I had exhausted every possible job lead I could find, and yet, I was still unemployed. The summer was over, and the kids were in a new school, back to the familiar routine. My wife was very busy with the kids and an ever-widening array of opportunities at our church. For all intents and purposes, I had been benched. God had called my number and sat me down. As I sat there and watched life seemingly pass me by, I grew more and more depressed.

I tried everything. If there was something to be done about my predicament, rest assured I did it. People came to me with ideas about jobs and career opportunities, and I chased every one of them. I began taking graduate courses at Spring Arbor University and otherwise occupied my time as a substitute teacher for the local school system. But I was disconsolate.

I prayed, but it seemed like I was just talking to myself. Many times I complained bitterly to my wife that my life had no purpose, and I had become a monumental failure. For a person who had been on the go his whole life, this was unbearable. For one who was accustomed to outworking the guy next to him, it was unsettling to realize that now I couldn't even work.

One night, out of desperation, I let loose with one of the most honest and sincere prayers I've ever prayed. I asked God a series of questions. "Why are you not listening to me anymore? Was I a better person last year when you heard me? Am I a worse person now? What is the difference? Is there something in my life that is hindering my prayer life? Is there 'sin in the camp' that I am regarding in my heart and not confessing?" I prayed those words late one night as I lay in my bed staring out the window, unable to sleep. The next day, God answered me.

I had just started working on this book. As I discovered, the process by which one undertakes the writing of a book involves other people. Pastor Howard Fuller had agreed to proofread parts of the manuscript. He had no way of knowing, of course, about my conversation with God that lonely night. However, one day soon after I received an e-mail message from him concerning the project. One of his concerns involved the portion of the book that would talk about my repentance. He was concerned that some folks might get the wrong idea and think I got away with some scandalous behavior without having truly repented.

I thought about his words all evening. It was an uncomfortable evening, to be sure. Only I knew the extent to which Brother Howard had nailed me. He didn't even know. I'm sure he thought I'd forgotten to mention it.

There was nothing in the book about repentance because I had never repented. I had never repented because that would necessitate being truthful. I went back to the time after my wife and I had gotten back together before we moved to Tennessee to take our first job. During that four-year span, I had been involved in several one-night flings while finishing college. These were in addition to the well-publicized affairs of before. I hadn't told her because they hadn't gone anywhere. I hadn't seen the need to unnecessarily hurt her again, not after what she'd already been through.

After graduating from college, we moved to Tennessee. I just breathed a sigh of relief that we had left my sordid past five hundred miles away. I figured I could start over without her ever having known about it. In other words, I adopted the philosophy of, "what she doesn't know won't hurt her." I had been so busy in Tennessee that I hadn't had the time to think about messing around. Furthermore, I grew spiritually during that time. Coupled with some maturity, I had been on my best behavior. Naturally, I thought I'd turned the corner and was now on the road to fidelity. I don't remember ever consciously thinking about the sin I had not confessed. I tried to bury it and hope it would never rear its ugly head again.

After the second affair had surfaced, my approach was to tell Katrina as little as possible. That course of action set me on a path to future sins against my wife that I was successful for years in keeping secret until that e-mail message from Brother Howard. It intersected with a change of my heart brought about by life circumstances. I was finally ready to do what I should have done years ago.

My wife had been away that evening. Before she got back, I asked God's forgiveness for my past sins of adultery. When she returned, we had a long talk. I told her everything. Instead of reacting with indignation, she was very calm and said something I still can't believe. She said she was sorry that I had been carrying around such a load of guilt for so long. We both agreed that but for the grace of God, we'd be another statistic littering the roadway of life. It was an amazing night.

I look back and see how my lack of repentance had such repercussions for me personally. I never realized what guilt can do to a person. It will make that person defensive and bitter. Anger will spill out at the slightest provocation. I remembered reacting angrily and accusatory toward my wife many times, and for what? I rationalized a reason or a cause at the time, but it was because every time I looked at her I felt guilty. Nobody likes that feeling or the person or thing that incites that feeling, so I lashed out. She told me later that our conversation that night had made sense out of many situations in our past that had, until that time, made no sense at all. I think she was almost as relieved as I was.

I also realized that my view of women was clouded by

my own history with them. The past occurrences had helped shape a view of women that wasn't at all Christ like. So many times in regular conversations, I had let slip a disparaging comment or two regarding women, and everyone would look at me, just staring. I'm sure I must have come off as a clod on more than one social occasion. Looking back, I can see a pattern that developed over the course of my life as it related to my interaction with women. This spilled over into my relationship with my wife and even my own daughters. I remembered my first relationship with Denise, how rebellion led that relationship into the abyss of purely physical attraction. Of course, it didn't take long for me to learn what I thought I valued in any relationship with a women. That was my start, and it only escalated from there.

I was so thankful that God answered my prayer. I had asked him to reveal to me anything that hindered my prayers. He used Brother Howard to do just that. Unloading that burden brought about freedom, just like he promised when he said, "the truth shall set you free."

The best part was that the relationship with my wife was now based on truth. There were no lies to remember and no past to conceal. There was no guilt or shame to run from or angrily react to. Everything was good.

Off to Egypt

I thought our move to Michigan would pave the way for our calling into full-time Christian service. However, we'd been in Michigan for about one year, and nothing had happened. If we had truly been obedient and were in his will, what on earth was taking him so long?

After investigating many different aspects of ministry, I realized that none of them appealed to me in the least. In fact, I felt unsuitable to be a preacher, a missionary, or a youth pastor. I asked myself, "if that's the case, why are we here? Did I not hear God speaking to me and telling me to leave Sycamore? Or did I take my family on a wild goose chase?"

The questions over this issue began to divide our home because my wife felt sure we were right where God wanted us. I, on the other hand, looked at our circumstances and began to panic. I couldn't see any answers. Thus, in my mind, we had made one monumental blunder by leaving a secure situation behind in Tennessee. There were some tense conversations as we tried to make sense of it all.

All the while, I had been dabbling with opportunities to get back into teaching and coaching. I kept abreast of the job openings back in Tennessee and had spent considerable time and energy scouring the area in Michigan as well. My mind was trying to figure out a possible solution to our situation, and it told me to go back the way I came.

The frustration I felt in my heart finally bubbled over one night. I came unglued during an argument with my wife. I blamed her for our predicament. My mother came to her defense, so I blamed her too. They encouraged me to stick it out and wait for God to open a door. I didn't think God was ever going to open any such door, so I determined to barge one down for myself. I informed them that from that moment on, I would be looking for a coaching job back in Tennessee. In my heart, our little walkabout in Michigan was over.

In the spring of 2005, I was offered the head-coaching job at Obion County Central High School in Troy, Tennessee. I interviewed with the search committee and thought, "there's *no* way I'm coming here." It was a good interview, though, and they called two days later to offer me the job. After thinking it over for a few days, I accepted the position.

Obion County reminded me of what Ninevah must have seemed like to Jonah. It was not an attractive place; West Tennessee is not the scenic part of the state, to be sure. The basketball program was a mess. They'd won in the past and then fired the coach responsible for their success. Since then, Obion had become a laughingstock.

It had lost sixty-six games combined in the previous three seasons. Coaches came and went. Parents, the school board, and community members beat a path to the powers that be and raised a ruckus every time the wind blew the wrong direction. The administration had no backbone, morale was low, and the team had a selfish reputation. All in all, Obion was a mess.

We had struggled financially for years in Cheatham

County because the pay was so low. Obion offered a livable wage. In fact, I was stunned when I heard the salary they offered. Suffice it to say, Obion offered a substantial increase over what we made in Cheatham County.

So, in spite of my initial impressions during the interview, we viewed the pay scale to be God's "fleece" and took the job with more than a little trepidation, I might add.

In Genesis, Abraham followed God's call on his life. In the middle of his journey though, he veered off the path and went to Egypt to avoid the effects of a severe famine. God didn't tell him to go to Egypt; he went on his own. The time in Egypt was almost disastrous. He had to plot and scheme to protect his wife from Pharaoh, and then, when the scheme was discovered, was forced to leave Egypt. He ended up traveling back to the very point where he was before his little detour. He then offered a sacrifice to God and resolved to finish the journey God's way. Like Abraham, I was trying to avoid the famine by taking my family to Egypt as a means of escape. Like Abraham, I wasn't patient enough to wait on God to fulfill his promise his way. We went in our own strength.

Famine & Pestilence

Less than one year later, on February 21, 2006, I found myself standing trial in the Obion County Courthouse in front of what seemed like the entire community. I was accused of assaulting one of my players. At the prosecution table sat Daniel and his mother. Behind them were the prosecution witnesses, mostly players from the team and their parents.

It was late in the season, and we had been struggling. In fact, the entire year had been one continuous battle. It started the first week on the job the previous spring. I had cut three seniors from the team during tryouts. As it turned out, I picked a gigantic scab off some wounds that had been festering a long time in the community when I cut two of those boys.

Both came from families of relative prominence. One's father was a school board member, and his grandfather was the town's mayor. The other's father was the pastor of *the* biggest church in town. Of course, the only one who didn't know any of this was yours truly. I later learned that these two families had exerted quite a bit of influence over the school system throughout the years. They were used to getting *what* they wanted, *when* they wanted it, and *how* they wanted it done. Who was this Yankee coach anyway, coming into *their* town and cutting *their* sons in *their* senior year? It seemed like I had stumbled upon a real life *Hazzard*, complete with a real life *Boss Hogg* or two.

I had been in my share of trouble when I was a student in high school, enough to know what the inside of a principal's office looked like, anyway. My high school experience paled in comparison to my year teaching and coaching in Obion County. After making those cuts, I ended up in the principal's office twice having to sign documents and listen to reprimands. As if that wasn't enough, I was then hauled down to the superintendent's office so he could have his turn. That all happened during the honeymoon period of my first week on the job. It was a peach!

After the season started, I fired the assistant coach I had inherited with the job. I had observed him being disloyal to the program, and more specifically, to me. I fired him during the Christmas break, which served as the mid-point of our season. Initially, the administration supported my decision, but it later changed its position when he filed a grievance against me. I was hauled into the principal's office twice more to be reprimanded yet again. Every time I went into that principal's office, he would have my file lying open on his desk. I noticed it kept getting thicker and thicker by the meeting. Foggy Bottom couldn't hold a candle to these pencil-pushers.

It was clear to me that I'd ruffled the wrong feathers from the start. When I first saw my teaching schedule at the beginning of the school year, I realized the principal was going to get the last laugh. I was the only teacher on staff without a planning period. It was a brutal schedule, but I was determined to push through and prove they couldn't break me.

In spite of all this, the team had been showing signs of

improvement throughout the year. We had doubled the previous year's win total and had a chance to advance to the region tournament for the first time in several years. The future looked brighter because we were competing with mostly freshmen and sophomores who had an eye toward what was to come.

I had run the And One drill before with this team during summer tryouts. I pulled it out again in late January, and that's when all hell broke loose. The drill has three parts. Each player must dive on the floor for a loose ball, get up and take a charge, and then score in the painted area against the coach. The coach uses a pad to cause contact and simulate a game situation where a player is fouled while shooting. The objective is to train the player to be able to focus through the contact and still score the ball.

Daniel was a senior who had lost his position to a freshman. He was angry about losing his spot and wanted to quit, but his mother wouldn't let him. He was the first player to go through the drill that day. He never finished. It took him several attempts to dive on the floor and get the loose ball. It took him several more attempts to take a charge correctly. By the time he dribbled toward me to score in the paint, he had already been on the floor a half-dozen times. He was not a happy camper.

I shoved him with the pad and he fell down. As he fell, he grabbed my shirt and pulled me on top of him. He wouldn't let go of my shirt, so I couldn't get up. I finally wiggled out of my shirt and got up. He just laid there, looking at me. I told him to get up and he did. He took his jersey off, threw it in my face, swore at me, and then quit. He spent the rest of practice standing against the bleachers while the rest of the team went through the drill.

None of this surprised me. Players had quit before at Sycamore when I ran certain drills. These kinds of drills are designed to weed out players who are not on board with the direction of the program. It's called addition by subtraction. Daniel hadn't been on board for some time now, and his attitude was polluting the locker room. I had sensed something amiss, so I had made the decision to run the drill and let it work its magic.

That night, Daniel's mother called my house screaming, "I got something for you, boy!" I hung up the phone realizing this was probably going to get ugly. Daniel's mother had a long, illustrious history in Obion County for making trouble for lots of folks. It was a matter of public record that she had sued former employers and had an attorney on retainer for all her litigation needs. As an African-American, she understood the power of the race card. The next morning, I was summoned to the principal's office, where I was informed that Daniel's mother wanted him reinstated to the team. I refused. I was dismissed from the meeting and went about getting ready for the day.

By third period that day, I realized the situation was now taking on a life of its own. The administration overruled me and reinstated Daniel to the team. I was called into the principal's office again and told to go home after fifth period. Later that night, the principal called me and told me not to come to school the next day. It had become apparent that the school system had unleashed Daniel's mother to do its dirty work by encouraging her to press charges against me. That way, they could be rid of the thorn in their side without getting blood on their hands. That was the last day I coached my team, taught my students, or set foot inside Obion County Central High School.

Meanwhile, during all this chaos, Katrina and I had noticed a lump growing behind Sammy's left ear. We first noticed it at Thanksgiving. We watched it for a while before taking him to the doctor. The doctor didn't seem concerned and told us it would resolve itself. Meanwhile, the lump grew until it was the size of a golf ball. Then it turned red. When a second lump began to form under his chin, we took him back to the doctor. They began treating him with medicine, but it didn't do any good. A third lump appeared between the other two, and we started to panic.

We finally found a doctor who seemed concerned about it. He began a series of surgical procedures to lance the swellings, drain them, and treat them with antibiotics. We went through several of these procedures, but the swellings would come back each time. Finally, he recommended we go to Memphis to a children's hospital for more comprehensive treatment. We had gone a couple times for tests so the new doctors and specialists could draw up a game plan for Sammy's treatment. They scheduled a surgery to take place two days after the infamous practice session.

It was a brutal day. We both struggled watching an otherwise healthy little boy go through such an ordeal, especially during the post-operation recovery time when the anesthesia wore off. He was so brave, though. Sammy had a personality that would light up any room. The nurses and doctors had a lot of fun with him.

After the surgery, we loaded Sammy back in the van and headed home. Little did we realize all that awaited us. When we opened the front door, an envelope fell to the floor. It was a letter from the principal informing me of my unpaid suspension from work. The words "unpaid suspension" hit like a hammer. A knock on the front door interrupted the silence. It was a sheriff's deputy with a summons for me to appear at my arraignment the following Monday. That was when I learned of the charges against me. Second-degree misdemeanor assault against a minor. That was a moment I'll never forget.

The lead-up to the trial was painful. Because I was a public figure within the community, and a polarizing one at that due to the nature of the charges against me, sides were drawn for battle. TV stations made me their lead story. I heard more about myself than I cared to hear on the radio, and I'm quite sure I was good for local newspaper sales. Simple things like going to the grocery store or attending church became an ordeal for the entire family. One morning as I was leaving the house to run some errands, I found nails spread across our driveway. On three separate occasions during this time, as I was jogging on the roadside, pickup trucks intentionally ran me off the road and into the ditch. We got a bitter taste of small town, "old South" hospitality.

Interestingly, I was approached three times before the trial by officials encouraging me to resign and give up the fight. I was promised that all the charges would disappear. One such encounter was initiated by a friend of the building principal, whose day job was unbelievably as an investigator for the sheriff's office. I couldn't believe nobody else thought his involvement in the case wasn't the mother of all conflicts of interest.

I still remember him showing up at my house wearing a navy blue jacket with "investigator" in bold, yellow lettering across his back. He made me get in his car and take a ride with him while he pretended to be my only supporter. He said he was there to look out for my best interests. His show of intimidation really spooked me, though. When we got back to the house, I half expected agents to spring out of my bushes with guns drawn, yelling at me to put my hands in the sky.

The other two meetings involved my attorney, the school superintendent, and the prosecuting family's personal attorney. They all wanted me to go away quietly like the previous coach had. My wife and I discussed the idea briefly before deciding it was not in our best interest to resign. We were sure I had done nothing wrong. Resigning would be tantamount to an admission of guilt. We wanted to fight to clear our name. The job itself was not a factor in the decision, as we both suspected it was permanently gone anyway.

The trial itself was surreal. My attorney drew up a list of defense witnesses he wanted to subpoena, and I added several folks to the list. I wanted the athletic director and the principal to appear so they would be forced to hear the whole story. All along, neither one had expressed any desire to hear my side. We never planned to use them in court, but by ordering them to appear as potential witnesses, they'd at least be forced to sit and listen to the truth.

In the end, the judge threw out the charges and dismissed the case. I was found not guilty. I can't describe the relief my wife and I felt as we heard the verdict announced. After the hearing, everybody went to the Mexican restaurant in town to eat. It was stranger than the trial. In one room of the restaurant sat the prosecution witnesses and supporters. In another room of the same restaurant sat the defense witnesses and its supporters. Some even mingled together.

The school system was forced to pay my salary through the rest of the contract once the trial had cleared me. They didn't want me around though, so now that my name was cleared, I resigned and was paid *not* to work. Meanwhile, the superintendent retired, and the school board denied tenure to the athletic director. Once the new superintendent was selected, he promptly reassigned the principal. The school board member who had started all the ruckus in the beginning was defeated in the next election. Most stunning, though, was the tragic death of the investigator less than a year later. He suffered a brain aneurism while attending a high school football game. During the subsequent year, I learned that he had used his position and influence to manipulate the investigation. He had been doing the bidding of his best friend, the principal. Six months after the fact, all the involved parties were gone.

Meanwhile, Sammy's surgeries had finally resulted in the desired effect. He had some scarring but was otherwise healthy as a horse.

Favor

God's favor spilled out on us as a family during the incredibly difficult 2005–2006 school year. When the situation looked bleak, I had trouble sleeping. I would get up, read from the Bible, and pray. The Holy Spirit led me to some wonderful passages of hope and promise. I would even type them out and reread them when I was discouraged. I remember vividly some of the promises he gave me during this time.

You find out who your true friends are during difficult times. While some abandoned us in our moment of need, God provided other folks to act as buffers. I don't know where we would have been without them, and I couldn't have picked more well-connected people to have on our side. It was a God-thing.

George and Jane McNeil lived down the road and adopted us early on. George was a retired law enforcement officer and had all kinds of connections to help us in our legal situation. Jane was a retired teacher in the Obion County system, so she knew the "lay of the land" from that perspective. O'Neil and Nancy Baker were prominent members of the community who had the resources and connections to help in more ways than I could ever recount.

Doug and Malinda Cunningham were big supporters of the basketball program who rallied to our cause. Greg

Ferguson was a board member who went far beyond the call of duty to aid and assist our family. His wife, Renee, was a source of encouragement to my wife on numerous occasions.

These folks dropped what they were doing and picked up the slack. They secured an attorney for us while we were in Memphis taking care of Sammy. One day, George showed up with a new freezer for our garage. A few minutes later, O'Neil showed up with more meat than I had ever seen in one place other than Wal-Mart. He owned a cattle farm and thought we might need something to eat. I referred to these wonderful people as "E.F. Huttons," people with no official title but lots of clout.

Groceries would appear on the back porch. We received cards and money from people we knew and some from folks we didn't know. The "E.F. Hutton's" arranged get-togethers to get us out of the house once in a while. They would call or stop by every day to check on us. I can't remember how many times Jane or Nancy would call from Wal-Mart or Sam's Club to get sizes for the kids because they were clothes shopping. I can honestly say that we had never before eaten or been clothed so well as we were during that time. God's favor was running down all over us.

God took care of our every need and then some. We never went without. Several Sunday School classes in our church paid our bills one month. The deacons paid our house payment for the month I had no income. When we needed tires on the van, they were provided. When Sammy's medical bills came due, they were paid. It was a time of supernatural provision.

After a time to unwind from the trial, we faced some big decisions as a family. We wanted to stay and fight to get my job back. The turnover in administrative personnel gave us hope that I could go back to work. But alas, too much damage had been done. We began to realize that the only way we could get my teaching and coaching jobs back was to hurt other people. My wife and I made a choice to give our case to God and let him restore us as he saw fit. The "E.F. Hutton's" wanted us to stay and battle it out, but we made the decision to leave quietly and let the healing begin. We put the house up for sale and prepared to move back to Michigan.

It was almost one year to the day when we were back in Michigan at my parents' house living as vagabonds again. The first time, I had been restless and driven to occupy myself as quickly as possible by securing employment and going to graduate school. We hadn't taken the time to be still and listen to God for direction, nor were we united as a couple on what, if any direction, we should go. Eventually, I got so antsy I took it upon myself to load up the family and venture into Egypt, otherwise known as Obion County. Now, like Abraham, we were back where we'd started, sitting in God's waiting room again. Only this time, we literally purposed not to move an inch until God had united our hearts and led us to make such a move. We put our eggs in his basket and decided to wait for his deliverance.

Giving Up and Giving God Room to Work

Some people learn things the easy way. Others require a knock upside the head, sometimes several knocks. I remember Coach Rice saying many times, "There's an easy way and a hard way. You just chose the hard way!" Looking back over my life, it seems like I've done a lot of running with those dreaded weight vests on, just like in my days with Coach Rice. It's made for some painful lessons.

During college, I wanted to be a professional basketball player more than anything. I would do whatever work was necessary to make that happen. If it meant working out eight hours a day, then that was the price I was willing to pay. Later, I wanted Sycamore to win a state championship so badly that I increased the strength of the schedule, instituted dawn patrol, and scheduled extra summer camps to bring it to pass.

I wanted to follow God's plan for our life after we left Sycamore. And yet, the plan had to follow a certain line of reasoning, namely mine. When the plan didn't reveal itself according to my timeline and things looked desperate, I stepped in and took over. I barged down a door to go to Obion County. Then, because I was going in my strength, I set out to prove it was the right move by creating a work load for myself and my players that an Industrial Revolution era sweatshop foreman would have been proud of. There was no time to build the all-important relationships; there was work to be done. The result? The season at Obion reminded me of the seasons before my first senior class at Sycamore. Dissension, disloyalty, hostility, anger, frustration, and disunity. I thought I had learned the lessons the first time, but evidently not.

In each case, God wanted to give me the desires of my heart, but he wanted the glory. In each instance, I discounted God and put together my own plan to make it happen. I failed on all three counts. In each case, there was a price to pay for my obsession. I almost lost my marriage during my playing days. I almost lost my team at Sycamore. I did lose my team and my job at Obion. It could have been much worse.

My misplaced priorities cost me time with my wife and children I could never get back. My schedule communicated a message to my family. The popular song "Cat In The Cradle" talks of a father too busy with his life and his dreams to be bothered with his most precious gifts, his family. The inevitable result was a broken relationship with his son, and worse still, the knowledge that his son was on the road to reproducing the same mistake all over again. That could have been me.

Thank God for his mercy, though. In spite of all my failings, he protected me as a teenager, salvaged a marriage that, in most people's opinions, was not worth saving, and protected my family from the whirlwind experience of Obion County. Furthermore, he graciously blessed me with extraordinary provision, gave health and healing to Sammy, and rebuilt so many fractured relationships in my life I lost count.

We spent most of 2006 and 2007 in Michigan going

around the mountain again. During that time, God stretched us. We were down and out. Then things got worse. Family members turned their backs on us, and people we thought were friends turned out to be the fair-weather types. As I remember that was the loneliest holiday season, as we struggled with one rejection after another. Meanwhile, our house back in Tennessee wouldn't sell. I couldn't find work of any kind. Money was running low, and I had no prospects.

I spent my time cutting wood, staining decks, cutting grass, clearing brush, and painting walls, anything to help out around the property. I took time to think, pray, and think some more. My wife and I took enough walks to qualify for an Olympic event. We prayed together. We cried together, and we talked. As time went by, we healed bit by bit.

I had resolved to let the coaching dream die. After what we'd been through in Obion County, I didn't want my family to hurt anymore. I determined to scratch out a living pig farming, if need be. I began to ask the Lord to show me a path to take. Katrina was doing the same. Way back when we left Sycamore, I thought I was being called into full-time ministry. After traveling downstate to Central Michigan University with Preacher Rick to do some open-air preaching, though, I realized that it was not my calling after all. I was conflicted, to say the least.

One day as I was stacking wood, I listened to a tape my wife had given me. I don't remember much about the message except a series of rhetorical questions: "What is your deepest desire, and where do you most feel God's favor? Are they one and the same?" It went on to explain that God puts those desires in our hearts, not us. He blesses and favors us when we do what he put us on this earth to do, because we are walking in obedience to his will. I stopped immediately, sat down on a log, and cried. I remember saying aloud something to the effect of, "God better not be pulling my chain." I knew what the deepest desire of my heart was, and I had indeed experienced what it was like to feel God's favor. There was no mystery in any of this to me. But there was no way I was going to spill the beans to my wife, because even the idea of coaching again would not be met with much enthusiasm, much less the unity for which we were praying. I didn't want to manipulate unity artificially, so I resolved to keep my mouth shut about the whole episode.

After I finished with the woodpile, I found Katrina inside the house. She asked me what I thought of the tape. I mumbled something and tried to change the subject. I was miserable. She looked at me strangely, though, with an intensity and a fire I thought had flickered out months before. She then dropped a bomb on my head. She said that *our* ministry was coaching. It was time to get back to *our* calling. After the words came out of her mouth, we both sat there for a moment, stunned, before hugging one another. Nothing else needed to be said at that moment. We just knew. It was one of the most special moments in our marriage.

In the ensuing days, I remember wanting to make sure. In fact, there was the fleeting thought that she was playing with my mind. Later that same week, I purposefully engaged her in several conversations, intending to trick the truth out of her. Surely she still dreamed of the day I'd go off to seminary and become a preacher. Nevertheless, she stuck by her words.

From that day forward, the seed had been planted again,

and it started to grow inside me. Since our commitment to each other was to be united this time before making any moves, we tested it by allowing some time to go by. We prayed for a confirmation, or like Gideon requested, a fleece. It came one evening in a conversation with my friend Dave. Unsolicited, he told me that he believed in his heart I should get back into coaching.

Later that week, another fleece arrived. A door opened for me to take a volunteer assistant coaching position with the local junior college. It was funny, actually, because I had stopped by his office to give him my résumé, and he wasn't there. I scribbled something on the top of my cover letter and slid everything under his door. He called two days later and offered me the position. Later, I found out that he never used that office. It was always locked and stuffed full of equipment. The lights didn't even work. He only discovered my résumé when he stepped on it while looking for an old scorebook. He already had two assistants, both of whom he'd coached. He knew them and was comfortable with them. Knowing how unusual it is for a college coach to let anyone "in the family" without some personal history, we could see God's fingerprints all over this. A minimum wage part-time job accompanied the position, so I began to re-enter life again, albeit slowly.

During the Israelites' walkabout in the desert, God provided for them in unique ways. Manna from heaven. Water from a rock. Shoes that didn't wear out. Feet that didn't blister. Relief from snake bites. We too experienced God's provision in unusual ways. Our house sold as we literally made the last payment we could have made. There was no more money to make any more house payments. We had enough money to pay bills through Christmas. We received enough monetary gifts during the holidays to carry us through the winter. Our tax refund carried us through the spring. The kids had enough hand-me-down clothes to carry them through the year. Nobody got sick or broke a toe. The car kept running. God's timing always kept us on edge, but in the end, he was faithful.

The Myers' family was a tremendous source of encouragement. We spent many nights over at their house just talking about our life. They prayed for us diligently and stood beside us like true warriors. There were many occasions when we felt like Moses with weary arms. Dave and Jenny were the ones holding our arms up most of those times. God gave my parents and friends like Dave and Jenny to sustain us because he knew we'd need them.

I had an identity crisis that year. I wasn't a teacher anymore. I wasn't coaching. In fact, my new identity was as an unemployed man, and according to the state of Michigan, a homeless one, too. I was tempted many times to give in to the feeling of uselessness. The enemy had a field day with me on that front.

However, I learned that my identity as a believer trumped all. My role as a husband, a father, and a friend gave me significance beyond what any career could give. I realized that my priorities needed to reflect these new insights.

I prayed and asked God to do the same kind of serious bridge-building between my kids and me that he had done between my wife and me. I didn't want my children to be as confused about whom they were and what purposes God had planned for their lives as I had been. I suddenly felt a strong desire to help nurture their gifts and abilities to help launch them into their purpose and calling successfully. I didn't want to send them mixed signals or confuse them because I was intertwining my desires for them with God's plan for them. For the first time, I became the spiritual leader in our home.

After three years in the wilderness, his favor showed up in a big way as an opportunity chased us down. A teaching and coaching position opened up back in Tennessee in March of 2007. We had prayed and prayed about an upcoming interview at a different school, and those prayers were answered. We didn't even have time to prepare for the interview because we didn't know about it until the day before it actually happened. The superintendent called me and requested first dibs in the interview process and then practically wouldn't let me leave the next day after five hours of interviewing. Campbell County High School hired me to be their new basketball coach that day. After all the rejection, we couldn't believe the lid had come off the basket so quickly.

After losing my job at Obion, I had interviewed for several head-coaching jobs in Tennessee, Kentucky, and Michigan. All passed me over because they were uncomfortable with the baggage I carried from the Obion situation. Every interview snagged on the same topic. We'd be sailing along having a great time and then pfft. You could almost see the air go out of the room. People would start looking around, at each other, at their watches, and at their cell phones. It seemed everyone wanted a current coach, not a former coach with failure on his résumé, to be their new coach.

Meanwhile, the state of Michigan was experiencing an economic calamity. All indicators had the Great Lake State ranked number fifty of all the states, even below Mississippi. Unemployment was rampant. Underemployment was an epidemic. Factories were laying off people everywhere. The "rust belt" was living up to its moniker.

People were leaving the state in droves. My daughter had a group of friends she ate lunch with at school that year in Michigan, and one day the topic of moving came up. Out of eight families represented at that table, she learned that folks were leaving for Europe, California, Ohio, Boston, and Tennessee. Only three families from my daughter's lunch table were staying in Michigan, and that was only because their fathers hadn't been laid off yet. The new state motto seemed to be, "Last one out, turn off the lights."

The schools were in terrible shape, so getting a teaching job was out of the question. Due to the mass exodus, enrollments were down across the state. The governor was threatening to cut school funding dramatically unless taxes were raised. For these reasons, we knew the open door to assist the men's basketball team and work part-time at Alpena Community College during the year had been a Godsend. Our three years in desert barrenness had changed our perspective. When the Campbell County interview happened the way it did, we both felt like rain had finally fallen on our parched and dried-out garden plot. It felt so good to be wanted and needed again.

As I reflected on what was happening, I was reminded of the passage in Revelations that speaks about God being the one who opens doors no man can shut and closes doors no man can open. Many times over the past four years, human beings had pulled every string they could to get us out of the wilderness. Every effort ultimately failed. In fact, Katrina and I eventually just smiled and nodded every time another well-meaning person would come by or call with a hot tip on a job. If human hands were involved, then we just figured it wasn't going to work, no way, no how. When the time was fulfilled, however, God made it happen in one day.

It seemed so long ago that I had begun praying for God to bless me, expand my territories, be with me, and keep me from evil. It had been four years since his word to me on the bus home from Bolivar about entering the promised land in spite of the obstacles that would be ahead. No, we hadn't won the state championship that year like I'd hoped, but God had answered my prayer.

My vision was quite small. It only involved my team. Ironically, the last three years had changed all that. He wanted to bless my relationships, my family, the work of my hands, my ministry, the dreams of my heart, my health, my future, and my finances. My wife and I decided to write vision statements based on the dreams and desires God had placed in our hearts. After a couple days to pray over our own statements, we compared them. The unity was striking. We were trusting God for many of the same things.

That's why I wrote this book. For years, I had harbored a dream to minister by traveling and speaking to people, to share my testimony as a means of encouragement. During my time on the shelf, I felt led to write about it and begin to make that dream a reality. Only he knows where it will lead. My role was to be obedient. It would be a gross understatement to say that my understanding of the prayer of Jabez and his word to me that night on the bus has changed only a little during the past four years.

One time during an especially discouraging week, Preacher Rick spoke some encouragement into my life. After listening to my story, he told me to think of three particular men in the Old Testament. Moses knew God had big plans for him. He tried to bring those plans to fruition by himself. It backfired, and he found himself in a desert for forty years in God's training ground. Joseph felt sure God had revealed to him through dreams that his destiny was significant as well. He bragged about it, ended up sold as a slave, and eventually landed in an Egyptian prison, no doubt wondering about those dreams he'd had years before. David was anointed king of Israel and had some other things happen along the way that must have convinced him too that he was going to be special. Yet he ended up hiding in caves and running for his life for thirteen years before the throne could be his.

All three had heard God speak the "what" to them correctly. None of them had a clue about the "how." It was demotion before promotion. In the end, Joseph *did* save Israel from the famine. Moses *did* lead the children of Israel out of Egypt. David *did* become Israel's king. They had to be stripped of their human resourcefulness first. They had to learn to rely solely on God. So he took all three out of circulation for a period of time to de-clutter their lives, their hearts, and their minds. He isolated them in lonely places to teach them to lean on him.

Michigan represented God's way-station for me and my family. It was a time of famine and loneliness. It was a time of preparation. Just like Coach Rice used to say, "there was an easy way and a hard way" to do the time. I chose the hard way and went around the mountain a few extra times by running off to Obion just like Abraham did when he went to Egypt. The year in Obion County only prolonged our stay in the wilderness because I was trying to circumvent the process.

Looking back, all the effort I put into trying to find work in Michigan was pointless. The jaunt to Obion County was a huge waste. God had given me a small glimpse of the future and led me to begin praying boldly for it. I heard the "what." I just didn't know the "how," and probably for good reason. I'm not sure if I had known that I would have still volunteered for the mission.

As the Israelites prepared to return to Jerusalem after being in captivity, they were faced with the daunting task of crossing dangerous territory full of bandits and thieves. They were concerned because they were loaded down with gold, silver, and other valuables. Ezra didn't want to ask the king for an escort because he had told the king that God would protect them. He and the people began to pray. Earnestly, they fasted and prayed more. Then they got on their donkeys and camels and moved. They didn't ask the king for backup or have any other fallback options in case God didn't deliver them from the hands of their enemies. They just moved and trusted. The God of Abraham came through for them, too, because they made it to Jerusalem safely.

Restoration, Reversal, and Reconciliation

As we prepared to move yet again, we decided to make a list of prayer requests relating to our changing circumstances. Before our move to Obion County, I purposed in my mind to demonstrate that I was acting responsibly by meeting all of our needs according to the wisdom of this world. This thought process led me to take out loans and make purchases that later became weapons turned against us. Having learned my lesson, this time we laid all our cares and concerns at his feet and waited for him to work.

First, we asked God to make a way for us to move together as a family. I had gone to Obion by myself for the first couple of months because it seemed like the smart thing to do. I figured I could coach the team, find a house by myself, and then bring the family down later. However, it was during this lonely time that I made a few decisions that proved costly.

As the time approached for us to move, however, we still had not received our answer. Less than one week before we were due in Campbell County, Katrina called about an ad she had seen in the local newspaper and discovered a man willing to rent a house to a family of six for a price we could afford. Furthermore, he offered to let us stay with him and his wife for a week or so until the house was ready and store all of our belongings in his garage. We had been concerned about the money we would have had to spend on a hotel room, a storage unit, and meals out while shopping for a place to live if we didn't have something lined up in advance. All those prayer requests were answered in one phone call.

Secondly, we knew I would need a summer job to carry us through until school started. I had mentioned this need in an e-mail to the superintendent of schools but heard nothing back from her before we moved. Once there, I got word that I needed to go see her in the central office about some paperwork. While I was there, she informed me that the system would pay me for coaching the team during the month of June as if I had been on contract the previous year, which, of course, I hadn't. I was stunned. Twice before, I had taken new coaching jobs and worked the first summer for free. In fact, the way I understood it, the system couldn't pay me until my contract started in the fall. In addition, she informed me of an opening during the month of July to teach adult education classes. It was my job if I wanted it. In one conversation, our prayers about summer employment were answered.

Thirdly, we knew that Katrina would need a job to help us get on our feet again. Since she had driven a bus when we lived in Cheatham County, we thought it was a good idea to get her license and have her drive a bus again. It was the only job we could think of that would pay decently, work out with my schedule, and still give her the flexibility to be at home with the kids. As we prayed about this need, we were also praying about a church home. We had visited several local churches and decided to settle on Cedar Hill Baptist Church. There were several factors involved, but we felt God leading us there.

Shortly after becoming members, the pastor approached me and asked if it was okay if he talked to Katrina about an opening they had in the children's department. They wanted her to be the new children's minister. The position would be extremely flexible and would pay better than bus-driving ever could. It all sounded great, but transportation was an issue because we only had one vehicle. Just a week later someone from the community called and told me to go down to a local auto dealership to pick something up. It was a van, almost identical to the one we had, but with fewer miles. All I had to do was sign some papers and go get some insurance, and it was ours. The Lord had come through again. We had a new church home, debt-free transportation, and a job for Katrina.

For several years, two of our children had been dealing with some serious wart issues. Everything we tried only served as temporary solutions. We had been praying about the kids and their warts. One day, shortly after we had moved to Campbell County, Katrina brought the kids to me and showed me where the warts used to be. They were completely gone! There were no traces, no scars, nothing.

I had injured my right arm and shoulder doing pushups while we were living in Michigan. I've never felt pain like that before. I couldn't grip anything with my right hand, and the pain never went away. I couldn't even block it out when I slept. We prayed about it, too. Again, shortly after moving the pain just went away. I woke up one day and it was gone.

The most amazing answer to prayer involved my team.

These boys, led by their parents, had walked out on the previous coach. One game night, the fans were all there, the opposing team was there, and the officials were there, but the home team never showed up. The coach had to recruit some kids out of the stands to field a team that night. Eventually, the elected officials pressured the appointed officials who ordered the hired officials to get rid of the coach. So I became the next coach. Interestingly enough, I learned soon after we moved to town that all the kids who had quit would be coming back out for the team. The previous coaching staff would still be teaching at the school, and many of the parents who had led the movement attended my church. Needless to say, the community was split right down the middle over the whole mess.

I began praying for wisdom. I firmly believed reconciliation was God's will. During the season one night after a game, I was driving home late after yet another disastrous performance. I cried out to the Lord for help, and he answered me later that night. I was reading about the Israelites and the Gibeonites in the Old Testament. Israel had made a covenant with the Gibeonites never to harm them. And yet King Saul had tried to wipe them out in his zealous desire to show himself "kingly." As a result, the Lord sent a severe famine upon the land. When King David learned about the breaking of this covenant, he set out to make things right with the Gibeonites. When everything was reconciled between the two peoples, God answered his prayer and healed the land. He sent rain and harvest where there had been blight and famine.

The next morning, I confronted the players with what I had learned. I told them that their actions toward the previous coach had been wrong and hurtful. They had circumvented the authority in their lives and had learned to be uncoachable in the process. Many times, we had prayed together as a team and asked God to bless and prosper us. As I explained to them that morning, God would not bless us and grant us a harvest until we dealt with the sin that brought the famine to begin with. I told them that I didn't care what they did, but as leader of this program, I was going to arrange a meeting with the previous coaching staff and the administration later that morning. I told them that I planned to apologize and ask forgiveness on behalf of the team. I wanted to set an example like King David did. He wasn't involved in the transgression, but he dealt with the fallout. I hadn't been there a year ago, but I was definitely involved in the fallout from the previous year.

The boys were crying as I talked. One of them got up, walked across the room, and hugged another player who had not quit the year before. The split between those who had quit and those who hadn't had left a division on our team. He asked forgiveness, went back to his locker, got on his knees, and began to pray through his sobs. I quietly left the locker room so they could have some privacy. Later that day, as I was meeting with the coaches and administrators, I learned that many of the boys had already approached them and asked for forgiveness. It was one of the most beautiful experiences I've ever had in coaching.

Later in the season, I had the occasion to confront one of the parents who had led the uprising. He was sensitive to my heart. In fact, he made a special point to come to the high school the next morning and ask the administrators to forgive him for his role in the matter. Because this individual was influential in the community, his actions had a ripple effect on other parents and members of the community. There was reconciliation and healing all around.

We finished the season with a 14–14 overall record, which was the first non-losing record the program had experienced in seven years. Not a juggernaut to be sure, but a start to something special.

Through it all, I've learned that the same God who came through for the Israelites time and again will come through for me and my family as we venture forth into every new challenge. When there was no hope for my marriage, God healed us. When enemies surrounded my family and tried to ruin us, God protected us. When the money ran out, God provided for us. When I was running through the streets of Fort Wayne, Indiana, while being chased by crazy group home people, God sheltered me and fought for me. Repeatedly, against all hope and logic, God has come through in the clutch. All the while, he's been chipping away a rough spot here and molding a new shape there to make me the man of character and integrity he can use for his kingdom. His grace truly is sufficient and will continue to be as he leads us on.

Contact Information

If you wish to contact the author, you may reach him at the following address:

Barry Jones
110 Teague Lane
Jakcsboro, Tennessee 37757
blj34_37146@yahoo.com
423-592-1971